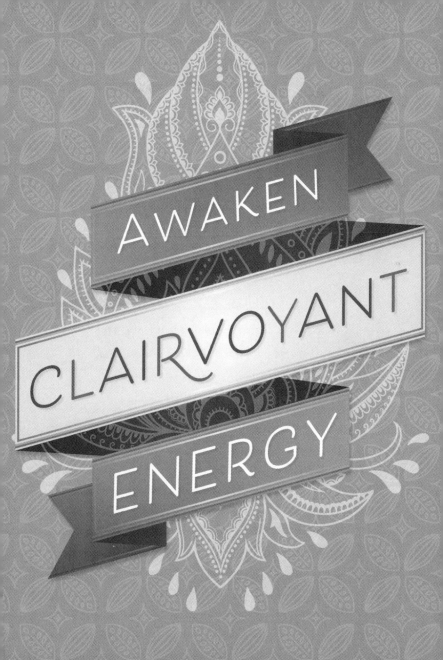

AWAKEN

CLAIRVOYANT

ENERGY

Cyndi Dale

(Minneapolis, MN) is an internationally renowned author, speaker, healer, and business consultant. She is president of Life Systems Services, through which she has conducted over 65,000 client sessions and presented training classes throughout Europe, Asia, and the Americas. Visit her online at CyndiDale.com.

Cyndi Dale's
--ESSENTIAL--
ENERGY
LIBRARY

AWAKEN

CLAIRVOYANT

ENERGY

CYNDI DALE

Llewellyn Publications
WOODBURY, MINNESOTA

FIRST EDITION
First Printing, 2018

Book design by Rebecca Zins
Cover design by Ellen Lawson
Illustration on page 36 © Mary Ann Zapalac
Eye of Horus symbol on page 18 from *Magic and Mystical Symbols
CD-ROM and Book* (Dover Publications, 2004)

Llewellyn Publications is a registered trademark
of Llewellyn Worldwide Ltd.

Library of Congress Cataloging-in-Publication Data
Names: Dale, Cyndi, author.
Title: Awaken clairvoyant energy / Cyndi Dale.
Description: first edition. | Woodbury : Llewellyn Worldwide, Ltd., 2018. |
  Series: Cyndi Dale's essential energy library ; # 2 | Includes
  bibliographical references.
Identifiers: LCCN 2017051358 (print) | LCCN 2017057865 (ebook) | ISBN
  9780738754802 (ebook) | ISBN 9780738751627 (alk. paper)
Subjects: LCSH: Clairvoyance. | Chakras.
Classification: LCC BF1325 (ebook) | LCC BF1325 .D345 2018 (print) |
DDC
  133.8/4—dc23
LC record available at https://lccn.loc.gov/2017051358

Llewellyn Worldwide Ltd. does not participate in, endorse, or have any authority or responsibility concerning private business transactions between our authors and the public.

All mail addressed to the author is forwarded, but the publisher cannot, unless specifically instructed by the author, give out an address or phone number.

Any internet references contained in this work are current at publication time, but the publisher cannot guarantee that a specific location will continue to be maintained. Please refer to the publisher's website for links to authors' websites and other sources.

Llewellyn Publications
A Division of Llewellyn Worldwide Ltd.
2143 Wooddale Drive
Woodbury, MN 55125-2989
www.llewellyn.com

Printed in the United States of America

Table of
-CONTENTS-

LIST OF EXERCISES   XIII

LIST OF FIGURES   XV

DISCLAIMER   XVII

INTRODUCTION   1

● ● ● ● ● ●
CHAPTER ONE

What Is Clairvoyance?   11

Ways Clairvoyant Visions Can Appear   4

Starry Night: Clairvoyance Makes
the Sights So Bright   13

A Nutshell History of Clairvoyance   15

The Six Styles of Clairvoyance   23

Energy Codes for Clairvoyance:
How We Make Pictures   33

"Cheat Sheet" of Visioning Forms
and Corresponding Chakras   40

CONTENTS

• • • • • •

CHAPTER TWO

Tools of the Trade: Preparing for Takeoff 43

Subtle Boundaries: A Clairvoyant's Protection   51

An Eye for Discernment: What's Involved in Clairvoyance?   57

Point of View: The Roving Eye   69

Questions for Assessing a Vision   75

"Cheat Sheet" Questions   77

• • • • • •

CHAPTER THREE

Classic Clairvoyance: Seeing the Sights Through Your Third Eye 81

Important Tips and Tools for Classical Clairvoyance   83

Ways to Perceive Attachments   89

Classical Clairvoyance: Inner Visions   106

Additional Tip: Visioning for Others   113

• • • •

CONTENTS

Classical Clairvoyance:
External Visions   118

Classical Clairvoyance: Nighttime
and Daytime Dreams   129

Additional Questions: Adding
to Your Queue   136

● ● ● ● ● ●

CHAPTER FOUR

*The Path of Prophetic
Visioning   139*

Bearers of the Light: Pictures
of Prophecy   140

How the Seventh Chakra
Sees the Sights   143

Sixth Versus Seventh Chakra Visions:
What's the Difference?   148

Additional Tip: Quartz It Up   155

Additional Questions: Adding
to Your Queue   156

• • • • • •

CHAPTER FIVE

Empathic Visioning: From Empathy to Vision 159

Empathic Knowledge: The
Two Main Sources 161

The Four Forms of Empathy: How
We Know What We Know 166

Additional Tips: Selecting a Focus
for an Empathic Sensation 172

Additional Tips: Receiving an Empathic
Message from Spirits 178

Additional Tip: Offering Insight to the
Owner of the Empathic Sensation 180

Additional Questions: Adding
to Your Queue 184

• • • • • •

CHAPTER SIX

Verbal Visioning: Where Words Meet Pictures 187

Capturing Meaning Through Words 188

CONTENTS

The Meeting of the Minds:
How Clairaudience Works
with Clairvoyance 194

Additional Tip: Using a
Scent or a Stone 201

Additional Questions: Adding
to Your Queue 202

● ● ● ● ● ●
CHAPTER SEVEN

*Clairvoyant Futuring: The
Art of Predicting* 205

Mirror, Mirror On the Wall: What's
in the Future for Us All? 206

The Four Futures 208

Future Factors: Distinguishing
Between Possibilities, Probabilities,
Certainties, and Warnings 216

Additional Tips: Making More
of the Future 228

Additional Questions: Adding
to Your Queue 232

● ● ● ●

CONTENTS

● ● ● ● ● ●
CHAPTER EIGHT

Healing and Manifesting Through Clairvoyance 235

Additional Tips: Healing Through
Clairvoyance 239

Additional Questions: Adding
to Your Queue 244

CONCLUSION 247

APPENDIX A:
QUESTIONS FOR CLAIRVOYANT ANALYSIS 251

APPENDIX B:
USEFUL INFORMATION 259

REFERENCES 263

● ● ● ● ● ●
EXERCISES

1 Technique One: Spirit-to-Spirit   45

   2   Awakening Your Third Eye
   Through Spirit-to-Spirit   49

      3   Technique Two: Healing
         Streams of Grace   53

4 Establishing Energetic Boundaries   55

5 Changing Visual Points of View   72

6 Classical Sixth Chakra Visioning   109

7 Reading Another's Auric Field   114

      8   Analyzing a Sign   124

   9   Seeking a Sign: The Everyday
         Vision Quest   126

10 Analyzing a Clairvoyant Dream   131

   11   Requesting a Clairvoyant
      Nighttime Dream   134

   12   Getting a Prophetic Vision   151

   13   Figuring Out the Ownership
   of an Empathic Sensation   169

   14   Visually Releasing the Empathic
      Energies of Others   174

15 Transforming an Empathic
Sensation into a Psychic Vision   176

16 Drawing Empathically: Releasing or
Transforming Empathic Sensations   181

17 Receiving a Psychic
Verbal Vision   196

18 Verbal Visions in the Environment:
Making Meaning of Them   198

19 Clairvoyant Foresight:
Seeing the Future   225

20 Clairvoyant Healing: Working
Through Your History   236

21 Manifesting and Magnetizing
Clairvoyantly   241

● ● ● ● ● ●
FIGURES

1   The Eye of Horus   18

2   The Chakras and Their
    Psychic Skills   36

Disclaimer

The information in this book is not intended to be used to diagnose or treat any medical or emotional condition. To address medical or therapeutic issues, please consult a licensed professional.

The author and publisher are not responsible for any conditions that require a licensed professional, and we encourage you to consult a professional if you have any questions about the use or efficacy of the techniques or insights in this book. References in this book are given for informational purposes alone and do not constitute an endorsement.

All case studies and descriptions of persons have been changed or altered so as to be unrecognizable. Any likeness to actual persons, living or dead, is strictly coincidental.

INTRODUCTION

I've traveled around the world to teach classes about energy healing and intuition. What's the number one request made by students? They want to become more clairvoyant, a term that means "clear seeing."

Clairvoyance is one of many mystical gifts—and what an astounding gift it is! Through clairvoyance, we perceive visions. They might be colorful, wild, scary, or black and white, but these images are uniquely able to provide insight, spiritual revelation, advice, and glimpses into the past, present, and future. These visions can be seen on your inner mind screen or even with your eyes.

Many people think that clairvoyance is relegated to seers, psychics, or gypsies, but it's actually innate to us all. As I'll relay in this book, everything is made of energy. Becoming more clairvoyant is simply a matter of learning how to better manage the particular energy that creates the kaleidoscope of images, sights, and visions that you can use to steer your life. As with any activity, being clairvoyant takes practice—and education. You'll get both in this book, which is the second in the Cyndi Dale's Essential Energy Library series.

* * * *

How clairvoyant are you right now? Maybe your ability is comparable to a tight flower bud: it's there but has yet to fully bloom. Perhaps your clairvoyance gift has already blossomed into a mature rose. Whatever the case, there is room to grow. In other words, this book has something for everyone, no matter your current level of development in the clairvoyant field. If you are already comfortable with energetic matters, you'll feel right at home. My energy-based explanation of clairvoyance, as well as the included practices, can easily and quickly become extensions of your established expertise.

If you are a beginner, learning the concepts and techniques might sometimes seem comparable to acquiring a new language. I encourage you to stay with it. Your growth potential is enormous, as are the benefits available to you on this path. What if you are an experienced practitioner? What's exciting is that I share one-of-a-kind processes that can be compared to panning for gold nuggets in a stream. You'll glean fresh perspectives and practical tips with information that is unique to my practice.

For everyone, spending real time activating and honing your clairvoyance will gain you more precise images, deeper understandings, and spot-on interpretations. Even better, you'll expand your clairvoyant repertoire, becoming adept at clairvoyant styles you might not even know exist—yes, there are six different clairvoyant styles or applications, and each accomplishes different goals. Some people are naturally talented in one style, some in several. For many individuals, accessing these various gifts is simply a matter of learning about and using them. In fact, a clairvoyant vision can appear through any of the means listed on the following page.

As extensive as this list is, it doesn't even begin to relay everything that clairvoyance can accomplish. For instance, this gift of psychic visualization can connect you with the deceased or a child yet to be born. It can serve as a spaceship to travel in between lifetimes. It can be applied to healing and manifesting, decision-making and problem-solving, and even something as mundane as figuring out what to feed your dog. It can assist you with separating your energies from others and help you attract more love into your life. As well, this versatile gift can provide images and insights that are literal or symbolic, related to the past, present, or future, or belong to you or someone else. Your clairvoyance not only enables you to see into—and through—all things physical, psychological, and spiritual, but to perceive the truth of yourself.

Ways Clairvoyant Visions Can Appear

- a vivid nighttime dream or daydream

- a spiritual revelation, shown in shades of black, white, and gray against a clear background or an etching depicting a person, object, or site

- feelings and other sensations that can be turned into psychic images

- colorful pictures or "movies" that spring onto your inner mind screen

- imaginative images such as emojis and cartoons

- signs and omens that appear in the environment

- words that write themselves on your inner mind screen

- a vision of something that has occurred or might happen

- orbs or spherical balls of energy catching the eye

- ghostly visitors seen with the eyes

- meaningful images intuitively drawn on paper

- landscapes and characters viewed while "traveling" outside of the body

I'm thrilled that you're reading this book, for it's ultimately a journey that can better every area of your life. I know. I've been enjoying this odyssey my entire life—and I love it. I employ my clairvoyance in everything I do, professionally and personally.

Professionally, I'm an intuitive practitioner and energy healer. As such, I have used my clairvoyant gift in every one of the 65,000 sessions I've conducted. Typically, every client session kicks off with a vision, which I usually perceive on my inner mind screen. Frequently I perceive an array of colors, which describe a client's personality and gifts, and then the psychic pictures start rolling in. I might envision a client's past life or peer into a possible future. I might envision the factors underlying an illness, get a warning about an addictive tendency, or figure out what is fun to them. I never know what I'm going to visualize, but it's always interesting.

Other times, my clairvoyance operates through my eyesight. I've perceived angelic forms behind clients and also looming shadows. I've seen clients' colorful auras and shining chakras. No matter what appears, I've learned to trust my clairvoyance and use the techniques showcased in this book to provide helpful interpretations.

My clairvoyance enhances my personal life, not only my work, as I frequently receive visions in my everyday life. One time, an image of my dog Honey popped onto my mind screen while I was running errands on an early Saturday morning. In the psychic vision, Honey was pawing at my son's door. As soon as I saw the picture, I knew that Honey was tattling: my son had overslept his alarm. I hurried home and found out that was the case. It was a good thing that Honey had reached out, as my son had to take his ACT test. As this example shows, our clairvoyance can be a vital informant for our routine lives. After all, we are on this planet in order to fully experience the extraordinary in the ordinary—and vice versa.

How can you best awaken and develop your own clairvoyant gifts? Step into my parlor—or the "classroom" that is this book—and find out.

In chapter 1 you'll learn the basics about clairvoyance. I'll first take you on a historical tour, revealing how clairvoyance has been used across time. Then I'll give you several examples of the six major types of clairvoyance. This sampling will suggest ways that you can apply clairvoyance in your own life.

Next, you'll be shown how clairvoyance actually works. Clairvoyance is an energetic endeavor. There are two major types of energy, subtle (psychic) and physical (sensory), and you'll learn more about them in this section. Both types of energy contribute to clairvoyance, which employs your physical body but also two different subtle structures called the chakra system and the auric field. One particular subtle center, the sixth chakra—also called *ajna* in Hindu and the third eye in colloquial language—has been linked to clairvoyance for thousands of years. As you'll discover, however, every chakra and auric field can be engaged to enhance your clairvoyant abilities. This fact will greatly magnify your clairvoyant powers.

In chapter 2 I'll reveal several tools of the trade. You'll immediately put these techniques to work to activate and employ your clairvoyant energy.

Thus prepared, you're ready to fully engage the six forms of clairvoyance, and chapters 3 through 8 are about doing exactly that. Within each chapter I present specific concepts and techniques for evolving one of the six clairvoyant aptitudes. You will learn how to cultivate a colorful vision, open to spiritual revelation, transform empathic sensations into pictures, access words and sounds through visual means, read and manage the future, and perform healing and manifesting.

Along the way I'll be helping you develop a set of questions you can use to cultivate, assess, and benefit from your clairvoyant visuals. In fact, the final list, shared in appendix A, will be comprised of the questions given at the end of chapters 2 through 8. By the time you are finished with this book, you will have learned about and implemented a broad range of clairvoyant styles and know how to work with each.

Ready to dive into the pool of spirit-knowledge that is yours? Then let's begin.

What Is Clairvoyance?

When eye specialists test our eyesight, they use specific tools and assess against measurable standards. It's harder to be this precise with clairvoyance as it is essentially a mystical or supernatural ability, but this complication makes our attempt all the more important. How can you develop an ability unless you can define it? How can you become better at something unless you can perceive it in all its many forms?

The purpose of this chapter is to make sure that you are clear about what clairvoyance is, how it appears, and what makes it work. Toward this end, I will begin this chapter by first whetting your appetite. The word *clairvoyance* means "clear sight," but this phrase doesn't completely encompass the gift. Right away, I invite you to perceive clairvoyance within a more colorful context.

Next we'll gaze at clairvoyance through the crystal ball of antiquity. Why do I want you to jump into yesteryear with me? All subjects are easiest to understand within a historical context, and clairvoyance is no exception. I think you'll be fascinated by this brief review of clairvoyance against the backdrop of time and find the few great clairvoyant sages you'll meet equally interesting.

One of the great "secrets" about clairvoyance is that there are many types or styles, which is the next exciting topic in this chapter. As you read through the overviews of the six main types of clairvoyance, I encourage you to reflect on which of the many styles you already have experienced and which ones you want to add to your wish list.

Finally, we'll look at clairvoyance through another lens: that of science. This "sharp right" will take us into the world of energy, for clairvoyance is mainly a function of subtle or psychic energy, although it also interacts with physical energy. After explaining what I mean, I'll introduce you to the two main subtle structures through which clairvoyance operates to serve its ultimate goal, which is to illuminate the brilliance of life. After all, is it not through the everyday that we express the light that we are? Is it not through our clairvoyance that we see the everyday in such a way that we desire to shine within it?

Starry Night

CLAIRVOYANCE MAKES
THE SIGHTS SO BRIGHT

Have you ever seen the Vincent van Gogh painting *Starry Night*? In it, turbulent swirls of bold colors and expressive images illustrate the moon in a starlit night sky. Van Gogh might as well have said that this painting was a product of his clairvoyance.

Van Gogh lived in the same physical reality as did his peers, but he saw—and illustrated—it differently. His interpretation has helped us all envision the sky, stars, and ourselves in a new way. This is one of the main reasons that people long to awaken or further develop their clairvoyance.

Universally, we all want to part the curtain of normalcy and discover what *really* lies on the other side. We want to change reality by viewing it differently. We yearn to grab ahold of a problem, crack its shell, and uncover the pearl inside.

Because of clairvoyance, we can also understand cofounding issues, ask a question and receive pictorial responses, and imagine a healing into existence. We can open to divine revelation, bond with spiritual guidance, comprehend our nightly dreams, manifest a desire, and understand events that are from the past, in the present, and related to the future.

Clairvoyance can accomplish these and many other goals because it is a psychic sense. Other words for psychic are *subtle* and *spiritual*. All these terms connote a visual sensitivity to energy that can be perceived by our inner eye as well as through our normal eyes.

When a clairvoyant image or set of images is noticed on the inner mind screen, it might look like something we would spy with our external eyes. Maybe a picture pops in of a child eating dinner or our mother cooking in the kitchen. Then again, an internal clairvoyant vision can also appear as a shape, color, movie, blur, symbol, black-and-white figure, or something even more difficult to describe.

The same is true when we're visualizing a psychic message with our normal eyes. We might perceive a ghostly form next to a friend or maybe a corona of colors around his head. It's even more likely that we will perceive the supernatural through the natural. For instance, I have a friend who knows that every time she spies a bluebird, she's supposed to eat. She has low blood sugar, and bluebirds prompt her to take care of herself.

Fundamentally, it's not the way a vision appears that makes it psychic or subtle or spiritual; rather, it's the meaning conveyed by the vision. If the supernatural is pictorially involved, either through the delivery or interpretation of the image, it's clairvoyance, one of the most important and validated mystical gifts of all time—and across time, as will become clear in the next section.

A Nutshell History of Clairvoyance

The history of clairvoyance is rich and complex, as evidenced by the variety of names associated with the gift. My personal favorite is a term I heard at a bed-and-breakfast on the Isle of Mann in Scotland, where I was staying on Midsummer's Eve several years ago.

Legend states that spirits walk the standing stone circles in that area on Midsummer's Eve. When I asked our hostess if she had ever seen these fairies, she replied, "Why, all the time." I asked how, and she looked at me nonchalantly.

"Obviously, I use the Sight," she replied. "Everyone on the isle has it."

Perhaps everyone everywhere has the Sight?

There are dozens of names for the clairvoyant ability. A sampling from across time and around the world includes the following terms: the second sight, the divine eye, the inner eye, the eye of God, the psychic eye, the eye of Horus/Ra/Wadjet, the spiritual eye, the mind's eye, and the eye of the soul. In addition, clairvoyance has been associated with labels associated with predicting the future, including *precognition*, which involves sensing the future; *foretelling*, which involves speaking the future into existence; *forewarning*, the process for perceiving upcoming difficulties; *foreseeing*, the seeing of the possible future; *foreknowing*, the empathic sensing of the future; and *futuring*, the term I'll most frequently use. Futuring encompasses all forms of sensing, knowing, speaking about, or seeing the possible future.

Other futuring terms that describe visioning during space-time travel include remote viewing, remote influence, astral travel, and remote journeying. All of these labels depict the ability to travel psychically or energetically to other places and spaces. Yet other language related to clairvoyance includes *retrocognition*, the ability to envision the past; *divination*, or the obtaining of psychic information; *aura reading*, involving the visual assessment of the energy field; *chakra reading*, the analysis of the body's energy centers; and *scrying*, the use of an item, such as a mirror, to view the future. These ideas will be further discussed within this book.

What are the labels used for individuals gifted with clairvoyance? The most well-known names include seers, oracles, diviners, visionaries, sybils, prophets, soothsayers, and augurs. Certain clairvoyant trades are also well known, such as palm or hand, tea leaf, and tarot card reading. In fact, some cultures employ parrots to determine the future. A parrot selects an inscribed piece of paper from a collection of papers and presto, you have an answer.

Worldwide, clairvoyance is associated with a subtle energy center called a chakra. Chakras will be described later in this chapter. For the purpose of understanding the contextual knowledge of clairvoyance, however, it's important to know that clairvoyance is most commonly linked to a specific subtle energy center. Located in the brow, this sixth chakra is called the *ajna* chakra in Hindu. Because it's an invisible and extrasensory eye, located between the two visible and sensory eyes, it's also called the third eye in dozens of cultures.

Many Hindu deities are decorated with a bit of red powder in this central forehead spot. Called a *tilaka*, this red dot is also pasted on worshippers during ceremonies. A similar custom exists in South Asia, where the third eye is decorated during rituals. This third eye area is also shown as a circle, gem, eye, or jewel in Buddhist, Tibetan, Jain, Taoist, and Japanese cultures.

In ancient Egypt the clairvoyant power was synonymous with the Eye of Wadjet. Wadjet, whose name is also depicted as Wadjyt, Wadjit, Uto, and Buto, was a goddess. The same clairvoyant eye, a symbol of protection, royalty, and good health, depicted in figure 1, was also linked with Ra and Hathor, other Egyptian deities.

FIGURE 1: *The Eye of Wadjet*
Also called the Eye of Horus and the Eye of Ra, this is an ancient Egyptian symbol that represents the clairvoyant powers of protection, good health, and royalty.

According to one legend, Wadjet was considered the daughter of the god Ra. Ra asked her to be his "eye" and find two beings lost in the seas. He was so thrilled when she successfully returned that he created the first humans from his tears. He then placed Wadjet on his head in the form of a cobra so she could always protect him. As his third eye, she is considered clairvoyant and all-seeing (Hill 2008, Hill 2016).

As implied, clairvoyance has been revered around the world. In ancient Greece, rich and poor alike consulted oracles, female clairvoyants who received visions offering advice from the gods. In fact, the oldest traditions in Tibet also employed oracles who spoke for the deities. These kutens, or mediums, when possessed by a deity, would channel prophecies. Over time, newcomers moved into Tibet from other countries, but the indigenous belief in psychic practices remained. Even now the Tibetans use divination and astrology in their everyday lives (Roney-Douglas 2012).

Politically, many ancient leaders employed clairvoyants to make important decisions. As a case in point, a movement called Lamaism emerged in China at the close of the eleventh century. Lamaism employed lamas, or Tibetan holy men, to administer Buddhist practices. Called "pastors of the soul," lamas were led by a "grand lama," as in the Dalai Lama. In ancient times, the Chinese emperor consulted the grand lama in all ecclesiastical matters, calling upon the Dalai Lama's "special eye" to gain insight and advice. Even now the current Dalai Lama is revered for his clairvoyant eyes (Bennett 1881).

Our ancestors' leaders—the smart ones—usually followed the sage advice of a clairvoyant, but not always. Perhaps you've heard of Cassandra, the ancient Greek clairvoyant who could foresee the future. Alas, she was doomed to be disbelieved. When she warned the Trojans that the Greeks would destroy them, they failed to heed her advisement, and her prediction came true. In came the Trojan Horse, and that was the end of Troy.

Yet another famous Greek clairvoyant from mythology was Tiresias, a blind seer. Well respected, he was unique in many ways. Legends state that he was born as a man but also spent seven years as a woman. Stories differ about how and why this transformation occurred, but many suggest that this conversion process left him physically blind, yet gifted with the ability to see into the future. Like other oracles, he often received visions directly from the gods. At other times he saw visions through other vehicles, such as in the smoke of burning offerings.

Religion is replete with clairvoyants, not excluding the Abrahamic religions. One noteworthy Judaic clairvoyant is the prophet Ezekiel. In the scripture devoted to his story, we read that Ezekiel was taken to the heavens to communicate with God. After his visit he delivered several prophecies that came true, including the fall of the great city of Tyre and the destruction of the Temple of Jerusalem.

Joseph is yet another well-known biblical seer. Known as the prophet who wore the "coat of many colors," a gift from his mother, Joseph was abandoned by his brothers and taken to Egypt as a slave. When locked in an Egyptian prison, Joseph was granted futuristic dreams from God. When these came true, the pharaoh rewarded Joseph with his freedom—and plenty of power and money.

There are countless other examples of clairvoyance in the Abrahamic religions. For example, during the 1400s Joan of Arc was struck by visions so pronounced that she led a revolution based on them. The prophet Muhammad, the founder of Islam, was famous for his interpretation of dreams. And Mormonism, a form of Christianity, began with one of the more unusual stories of clairvoyance: in the 1800s Joseph Smith was directed by the angel Moroni to a hill near his home. There he found a buried box that contained golden scrolls. Over time, Smith translated the scrolls using a seer stone that he placed in his hat.

Other famous clairvoyants include French seer Michel de Nostredame, or Nostradamus, who in 1550 started publishing visions about the future. Many of his predictions have seemingly come true, such as the occurrence of World War II and the rise of ISIS. Edgar Cayce, who was born in the 1800s, worked as a healer, but his visions also addressed topics ranging from the stories of Christ's various incarnations to the existence of Atlantis. Baba Vanga is yet another famous clairvoyant. A Bulgarian woman born in 1911, she was often visited by invisible creatures who told her about the future. Her visions, which began when she lost her eyesight, have been known to be accurate.

During my studies and travels, I've yet to come across a culture that doesn't somehow embrace the existence of clairvoyance. In Peru I participated in healing ceremonies in which the only goal was to receive psychic visions. In Lakota rituals I followed the lead of a medicine man, who would encourage participants to receive visions from the ancestors. I partook of similar processes in several Central and South American villages, as well as in Russia. Deep in the Sahara, I visited an old Jewish library surrounded by sand. The guide there explained that the rabbi who last tended to the library had used many of the same predictive techniques as employed by earlier Jewish holy men, including the employment of special dice designed to determine God's word. And even in shopping malls in America I have come across clairvoyants offering tarot card or psychic readings. Universally, humans believe in—and engage with—their own and others' clairvoyance.

All over the world, cultures cultivate visions, and not only because they always have. They do so because there are sights to see—and feel, know, and share. Because of the fluidity of clairvoyance, it's important to expand our definition of it from simply being about "clear sight" to being inclusive of all sorts of psychic visioning—in fact, the six specific types of psychic visioning you'll learn about next.

The Six Styles of Clairvoyance

As you can perceive from the many examples of clairvoyance I've already presented, clairvoyance expresses itself in many ways. I've organized these ways into six categories that match the subjects of chapters 3 to 8. In these later chapters, you'll dig into each of the clairvoyant styles and also practice them. The styles are as follows.

1: Classical Visioning

This style of clairvoyance is the most well known and involves the ability to perceive visions that are colorful. These pictures appear in one of three ways:

INNER VISIONS: These clairvoyant images appear in the mind's eye as if drawn by supersonic crayons. A clairvoyant picture can stand alone or several images might be strung together, much like a slide show or a movie. The images can be interpreted literally or figuratively. They might also depict the past, present, or future and involve a variety of shapes and forms.

EXTERNAL IMAGES: As already expressed, some clairvoyant visuals can be seen with our physical eyes. The well-known art of reading an aura, the energies surrounding a living being, is often conducted via normal eyesight, as is spotting otherworldly spirits and guardian angels. Omens and signs can also appear in the environment via a meaningful message formed by the letters on a license plate or a billboard or through the sighting of an animal or bird.

DREAMS: Clairvoyance is an integral part of dreamtime. Anytime you are dreaming visually, you
are being clairvoyant. Nightly dreams often
contain psychologically based communications
but also can involve interactions with other
souls or beings, who might show up to instruct
or advise. We can also experience clairvoyance
via our daydreams. As our mind wanders, we
might replay an event that's already occurred or
trip into a possible future. In particular, future
daydreams can help us work through issues
that impede progress or assist us with making
important decisions.

Classical clairvoyance is the most popular of all the
clairvoyant processes and most likely the one you've most
frequently experienced. The trick with classical clairvoyance is arriving at the correct interpretation of a vision.

I've learned that I must trust and "go with" whatever
is being presented to me. This isn't always easy or comfortable. For example, I was once conducting a client session with a woman named Janice. The only image I psychically received was the picture of mud with two dollar
signs sticking out of it. That's it: an image of mud and
money.

Since nothing else appeared, I was forced to present this image to my client, although it made absolutely no sense to me. Janice laughed and explained.

"I took a huge risk and hired an expensive landscaper to redo my entire lawn. My goal is to sell the house when he's done." She paused. "He insists I'll double my money. I guess I will!"

A few months later, Janice sent me an email. She had more than doubled her landscape investment when her house sold.

Most of the individuals I know rely on external signs and omens, although they may not have branded these phenomena as clairvoyant. When a good friend of mine was trying to decide whether to move to the West Coast or not, he started spying eagles. He lived in the Midwest at the time. The eagles were always flying west. He moved west.

And who amongst us hasn't relied on our nightly dreams or daydreams to better understand ourselves or to make a decision? Classical clairvoyant dreams tend to be vivid and colorful. One of my favorite stories that showcases the importance of clairvoyant dreams relates to an eighty-year-old man who had attended one of my seminars.

When I was discussing dreams, he raised his hand and shared that since he had undergone a near death experience, or been declared dead but returned to life, his nightly dreams included visitations by angels. His wife, who sat next to him, confirmed that her husband often awoke from these interactions with messages for her and their children. Every message was wise and meaningful, although once, the angels had insisted that he tell one of their daughters that she should refrain from wearing red. It "wasn't her color."

As you can see, classical clairvoyant visions can inform us about the details of life, great and small. You'll learn all about classical clairvoyance in chapter 3.

2: Prophetic Visioning

While classical clairvoyance usually appears in Colorama complexity, prophetic versions of clairvoyance are versions of black, white, and gray. They provide spiritual revelation about—or an evaluation of—a situation. The black-to-white continuum indicates negative to positive energies respectively, with gray being in between. When gray appears, I assume that something is hidden from sight.

Prophecies steer us toward enlightenment, the state of living in oneness with the Spirit. They also help us figure out if an activity or attitude will help us fulfill our destiny. For instance, I once worked with a client who asked if she should enter an arranged marriage in her home country. I asked what would happen if she agreed to the marriage. The ensuing image was of her wearing a gray dress surrounded by dark shadows. Despite this ominous warning, my client flew to Pakistan and married the man, only to return a year later, divorced. The man had been abusive.

Details about prophetic visioning are covered in chapter 4.

3: Empathic Visioning

Clairvoyant images don't always start pictorially. They can arise from empathic information, which enters our system as feelings, sensations, or awareness. However, we can transform kinesthetic knowledge into classical or prophetic images, therefore turning an impression into a visual. This resulting image will provide insights as to the nature of a sensation or awareness.

For example, one of my clients had been waking every morning for several months with a burning sensation in his hand. After checking the symptom out with several medical professionals, he came to me. I had him turn the pain into a picture, using the method you'll learn in chapter 5. He viewed himself painting. Apparently he had ignored his artistic bent to enter law school in order to please his father. As soon as he started painting again, the pain stopped.

Sometimes the empathically sensed impression isn't our own. Many sensitive people absorb others' physical issues, feelings, thoughts, and needs. In this case, we can use clairvoyant visualization to separate our own from another's energy and then return the energy to its true owner. You'll learn all about empathic sensations and the application of clairvoyance to work with them in chapter 5.

4: Verbal Visioning

Clairvoyance can be combined with clairaudience, another famous mystical ability, to access words, lyrics, and other verbal means of communication. Clairaudience means "clear hearing." Although this book isn't about clairaudience, clairvoyants can tap into their clairaudience to assist in their visioning efforts. For instance, in your mind's eye you might envision captions on a picture or the words of a poem.

I once employed verbalization to figure out the meaning of a recurring dream. The dream always ended in me buying something on the internet—but I never knew what. I meditated and asked for a caption. The word *rug* flashed into my mind in red letters. Since that time I've been purchasing all my rugs via the internet at great savings. After all, with kids and dogs, my rugs get a lot of wear and tear. You'll be shown a simple process for blending your clairaudience and clairvoyance in chapter 6.

5: Future Visioning

As I'll discuss in chapter 7, there are many names for the clairvoyant gift of foreseeing or the divulging of future events, or futuring. There are also many types of future images, such as those showcasing possibilities, probabilities, warnings, or certainties. The entirety of chapter 7 is devoted to this age-old use of clairvoyance, through which foresight is available through the use of classical, prophetic, empathic, or verbal visuals.

Futuring is a tool available to everyone, not only individuals who use this skill in their work, as do I. In fact, a friend of mine was once spared a traffic accident because she dreamed about a car wreck on a specific highway. The next day she took a different route to work. Later, she learned that there had been a fatal accident on the highway at the time she would have been traveling on it.

6: Healing and Manifesting

Some of the most ancient and well-advertised applications of clairvoyance are for healing and manifesting purposes. Healing and manifesting are two sides of the same coin. In general, healing occurs through releasing energy and manifesting operates by attracting energy.

More specifically, healing involves creating beneficial change. Clairvoyance is a master tool for performing healings, whether they involve physical, psychological, or spiritual shifts. For example, I have a friend who can see underneath another's skin and watch the flow of fluids. Wherever there is an impediment, she envisions a clearing of the block. Her clients immediately feel better.

Manifesting involves using visualization to attract what we need into our lives. Depending on your clairvoyant style, you can learn how to picture—or draw—what you desire and open to receiving it. You can even transform a feeling, desire, statement, or another form of knowing into a vision to concentrate on. I once worked with a woman who was sure she wasn't clairvoyant, but she was willing to try anything to attract a life mate. I had her sense what she'd feel like with the right man and then convert the sensations into a symbol. She selected a white cross. She would picture this image daily. Within a few months, she met an incredible man. He was a pastor and wore a white cross.

———

Are you surprised by the diverse activities covered by the umbrella term "clairvoyance"? You are bound to be talented in at least one style; why not develop the others? You can also amplify clairvoyance with specific tools, including stones, oils, and even food. Clairvoyance also can be enhanced with the proper understanding of shapes, symbols, colors, and the other pictorial ingredients. These and other qualifiers, or interpretive factors, will be described in ensuing chapters. As with any gift, techniques that might feel strange at first can be mastered with education and practice.

Right now, you are probably feeling pretty excited about what you can do with your clairvoyance. You'll feel even more able to develop your gift after learning how clairvoyance works, which explains why clairvoyance is so universal. The truth is that humans are encoded for psychic visioning. The only complication in describing the process is that it involves two interactive anatomies.

Energy Codes for Clairvoyance
HOW WE MAKE PICTURES

The gift of psychic vision is best explained by the existence of two different yet interdependent human anatomies. These are the physical and subtle anatomies, which could also be called the sensory and psychic anatomies. Together, these systems underlie our ability to be clairvoyant.

You already know the basics about your physical anatomy. Your physical anatomy comprises many parts, including organs, channels with fluids (like blood and lymph vessels), and electromagnetic and sound fields. Cumulatively, physically based structures process information, take in and distribute fuel, and connect the body to the world.

Your other anatomical system is the subtle body, also called the subtle energetic anatomy. Like your physical anatomy, your subtle body is also comprised of organs, channels, and fields. The specific labels for these three structures are the chakras, meridians or nadis, and the auric fields, respectively. These structures, like their physical counterparts, deal with information, assure nourishment, and manage worldly interactions. The main difference between these anatomies is the nature of the energy being processed.

· · · ·

Energy is information that moves. Everything is made of energy, whether that energy forms a doughnut or an idea. However, there are two fundamental types of energy. Physical or sensory energy is measurable and operates within a restricted band of frequencies. This is the stuff that we can see, hear, touch, smell, or taste—hence the label "sensory." Psychic or subtle energy, on the other hand, operates outside of the narrow box inhabited by physical energy. It's just as real as physical energy; in fact, it often can be understood through the physical senses. Subtle energy, however, moves faster or slower than physical energy does, which is why subtle energies are often termed the basis of our "sixth sense." In short, we have one anatomy to manage our sensory knowledge and another to govern our extrasensory activities.

Both anatomies work together to create clairvoyant visions. Sensory visions start when light passes into the eyes. The eye's rods and cones send the light to the brain, which interprets the light impulses based on memories and mental programs. You now spy an image. Note that the eyes are merely a starting point; the brain actually decides what you "see."

How do you perceive a psychic vision? The process is similar to the one that formulates physical sights, except that the entry point for the information is different. Psychic energy doesn't come in through the eyes alone, although you can receive spiritual messages via your normal eyesight. Rather, subtle energy typically enters the body through two of the three main subtle structures, the chakras and auric fields. (The subtle channels also play a role, but not directly. Rather, they distribute energies through the body.)

Chakras are subtle energy organs that lie inside or right around the material body. There are seven in-body chakras, each of which anchors in the spine, interacts with an endocrine gland, and regulates a specific set of physical, psychological, and spiritual concerns. Though they are subtle organs, chakras are able to convert subtle energy into physical energy and vice versa. They can do this because they both generate and operate on waves of electromagnetic activity, or light, and sonic waves, which create sound. There are literally no boundaries to what light and sound can do—and communicate—especially when operating at subtle levels.

Every chakra forms an auric field, a band of energy that surrounds the body. These various fields compose what's called the aura or the auric field. The individual fields are also called auric layers. The auric fields lay atop each

Seventh Chakra—White (Violet)
   Top of the crown
   Spirituality
   Gift: Prophecy

Sixth Chakra (Third Eye)—Violet (Indigo)
   Forehead/brow
   Insight
   Gift: Clairvoyance

Fifth Chakra—Blue
   Throat
   Communication
   Gift: Verbal/clairaudience

Fourth Chakra—Green
   Heart
   Love
   Gift: Relational empathy

Third Chakra—Yellow
   Solar plexus
   Mentality
   Gift: Mental empathy

Second Chakra—Orange
   Abdomen/sacral area
   Emotions
   Gift: Emotional empathy

First Chakra—Red
   Hips/base of spine
   Physicality
   Gift: Physical empathy

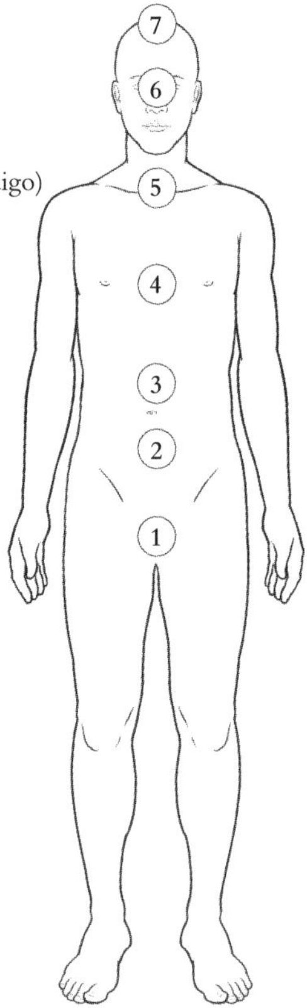

FIGURE 2: *The Chakras and Their Psychic Skills*

The seven in-body chakras are labeled in numerical order from the base of the spine upward. Each subtle center is anchored in the spine, regulates a bodily region, serves a higher mission, and can be perceived as a color. The main color of each chakra is also listed. The sixth chakra is usually considered violet and the seventh chakra is white. Another alternative preferred by experts who follow a rainbow sequence of colors, indicated in parentheses, assigns indigo to the sixth chakra and violet to the seventh.

* * * *

other, graduating from the densest to the most ethereal, and provide protection, boundaries, and filtering. As are their corresponding chakras, the auric fields are a product of light and sound. These fields are particularly important in terms of psychism because each field runs on the same frequency as does its partnering chakra.

Basically, when a psychic message comes our way, it is picked up by the auric field that matches its frequency. In turn, the field passes the data into its fellow chakra. The chakra, which stores information pertaining to its purpose and functions, helps interpret this incoming missive, but it also sends the data up the spine to the brain, which adds its own spin. The brain will help decide what to do with this message. Psychic messages created within the self are sent into the world through the same mechanics. The brain and/or chakra generates a message, which is passed into an auric field by its corresponding chakra. As you can see, the psychic process is a true melding of the physical and subtle anatomies.

Every chakra has several specialties, picking up on and working with specific physical and psychic energies. As you can see on figure 2, the first chakra, located in the hips, manages sensory energies related to that bodily region. The first chakra is also in charge of physical

* * * *

empathy, the ability to psychically sense what's occurring within all parts of our own body, but also in others' bodies. As per its intuitive faculties, the second chakra, in the abdomen, is emotional empathic. And the sixth chakra—the one known as the third eye—manages and creates psychic visions.

What this means is that when the data that makes its way to your sixth chakra through your sixth auric field is sent to your brain, it is deciphered visually on your mind screen and you perceive a psychic image. Your sixth chakra can also receive information from the various parts of your own body, sub-aspects of your personality (such as an "inner child"), other chakras, and your soul. You can also send psychic visions into the world, which others can respond to. As well, information that begins as an image perceived with your physical eyes might be loaded with subtle messages, which your brain stands ready to interpret.

While most esoterics associate clairvoyant images with the sixth chakra, many experts anchor it in the seventh chakra. The sixth chakra is linked with the pituitary gland and the seventh chakra with the pineal gland. There are many valid reasons to plant clairvoyance in the pineal rather than the pituitary gland. The pineal gland is a highly important organ, producing hormones regulating sleep and mood but also substances that induce states of higher consciousness. One example is N–dimethyltryptamine (DMT), which is a psychedelic compound associated with hallucinations and metatonic experiences. Personally, I link classical visioning with the sixth chakra and prophetic visioning with the seventh chakra. Both chakras and their corresponding glands are visual but create different types of images.

In fact, every in-body chakra is available for the production of visions, as you'll learn in chapters 3 to 8. It's simply a matter of mechanics, or the passing of psychic information from a non-visual chakra to a visual chakra. On the following page is a "cheat sheet" that relates the six basic forms and functions of visioning to their corresponding chakras.

―――――

Are you ready to get on the road and start putting all this information to work? We'll do exactly that in chapter 2.

"Cheat Sheet" of Visioning Forms and Corresponding Chakras

CLASSICAL VISIONING: Accomplished through the sixth chakra.

PROPHETIC VISIONING: Performed through the seventh chakra.

EMPATHIC VISIONING: Involves transforming first, second, third, and fourth chakra information into sixth or seventh chakra visions.

VERBAL VISIONING: Involves changing fifth chakra verbal information into sixth chakra pictures.

FUTURE VISIONING: Involves turning any chakric message into futuristic images.

HEALING AND MANIFESTING: Involves applying sixth or seventh chakra images to create beneficial change.

* * * * * * *

Summary

Clairvoyance is the art of psychic visioning. It is a long-standing and renowned mystical gift that has been accepted, employed, and enjoyed around the world. In fact, there are six main types of and uses for clairvoyance, which are classical clairvoyance, prophecy, empathic visioning, verbal visioning, future visioning, and healing and manifesting.

No matter its appearance or function, clairvoyance is an energetic activity, with "energy" defined as information that moves. The visions are created partially by the physical body and also by the chakras and auric fields, two of the subtle energy structures that process subtle as well as physical energies, converting each into the other. Because of this, clairvoyants can perceive psychic messages on their inner mind screen but also with their physical eyes.

While clairvoyance is primarily based in the sixth chakra, located in the brow, psychic images can also be formed from information available to the other chakras. You'll learn more about these transformational interactions and how to conduct them later in this book.

* * * *

CHAPTER TWO

Tools of the Trade
PREPARING FOR TAKEOFF

It's far easier to become an expert at a subject if you have the right tools, complete with instructions. The purpose of this chapter is to equip you with the basic concepts and techniques required to become a master clairvoyant.

Many people keep the best for last; not me. Right off, I'm going to teach you the most important technique that you need to know. Called Spirit-to-Spirit, this process will assist you through every clairvoyant endeavor. After I relay this practice, I'll put you to work by walking you through Spirit-to-Spirit in an exercise designed to awaken your sixth chakra, the home of the most colorful psychic visions.

Next, I'll discuss the all-important matter of subtle energetic boundaries. The more parameters you establish, the safer you are. The more secure you feel, the more expansive your clairvoyant gifts can afford to be. After our boundary conversation, I will acquaint you with the second most vital clairvoyant practice, which I call Healing Streams of Grace. You'll combine Spirit-to-Spirit and Healing Streams of Grace to cleanse and create boundaries. Both techniques, Spirit-to-Spirit and Healing Streams of Grace, are more fully described in *Subtle Energy Techniques,* the first book in this series.

Now for the nitty-gritty: How can you figure out what clairvoyant images mean? You "qualify a vision," or assess the factors involved in the vision. Most commonly, you have to contextualize the vision and figure out what each component means. Steps include figuring out if the vision is being received voluntarily or involuntarily (sought out or simply given) or descriptive or prescriptive (providing raw data or guidance).

With this knowledge in mind, you can hammer out additional factors, such as deciding if the vision is literal or metaphorical, determine the vision's source, and assessing point of view. In addition, you might distinguish which of three basic time periods are involved and more. After explaining these concepts, I'll provide a set of handy questions that will help you decipher a clairvoyant perception and search for additional insights. But first, let me introduce you to the number-one technique involved in clairvoyant interactions.

Technique One
SPIRIT-TO-SPIRIT

Spirit-to-Spirit is a three-part process that accomplishes several goals in relation to clairvoyance. It calls forth only the highest visions and interpretations, it allows you to interact with only the best parts of others, and it surrenders the entirety of a clairvoyant process to the only completely trustworthy source or guide: the Spirit. "The Spirit" is the term I use to describe the Holiest of Holies, which you might call Christ, God, Allah, Kwan Yin, the Goddess, the Holy Spirit, the Universe, the Divine, or even the Goodness in Humanity. After the Spirit takes over your clairvoyant process, it might turn the reins over to divinely approved spiritual guides or even to your own memory banks. The point is that it's always best to operate from the top down rather than from the bottom up.

Spirit-to-Spirit can be used when meditating, praying, or asking for a vision. You can also use it to gain knowledge of a vision you have received previously. It can be applied to any of the six clairvoyant styles, and, no matter what, it invites only the most positive outcome for any clairvoyant process.

The method is simple and involves these three steps:

STEP ONE: **Affirm Your Personal Spirit.** Your spirit is your essential self, the eternal part of you that has existed since time began. Your spirit is loving and prudent and is only going to let you receive, create, or send clairvoyant perceptions that will be safe and healthy for you on every level, including physically, psychologically, and spiritually. Sometimes our less wholesome aspects might indulge in less than savory or unhealthy visions, but that's not the case with our spirit, which will only interact intelligently.

To conduct this step, it's helpful to create an image or symbol you can use when performing Spirit-to-Spirit. You might envision yourself as an angel, star, light, flame, bird, or flower. Select a picture that assures you only your highest and wisest self is acting clairvoyantly.

Step Two: **Affirm Others' Spirits.** This step guarantees that you're only going to mingle with the most conscious part of others, whether they are people, animals, otherworldly beings, or any other entity or force. Why is this important to do? There are negative aspects of other people and beings, which often can be intrusive clairvoyantly. Step two of Spirit-to-Spirit makes sure you only communicate with the best part of a person or group you're interacting with, as well as their invisible connections. As with the previous step, you might want to create a picture, image, or color to hold in mind when acknowledging others' spirits. For instance, you can envision others as angels or beings wearing white cloaks.

Step Three: **Affirm the Spirit.** Through this step, you are surrendering all clairvoyant activity to the Spirit. This allows the Spirit to do the following:

- create a vision meaningful to you
- only allow you to receive visions appropriate for you

- protect you from inappropriate or harmful visions or visual sources
- protect you from any intrusions, interference, or manipulative entities, people, or energies
- shift feelings, bodily sensations, verbal insights, etc., into visions
- allow the alteration of a vision so as to better understand it
- send visions for the purpose of healing others or manifesting desires
- provide accurate interpretations of the vision

To acknowledge the Spirit, you can create a picture that will do the job for you. Many people like to use a visual such as a white flame, a dove, Christ, the Buddha or another iconographic image, or the sun. Select a depiction of the Spirit that suits your religion or beliefs.

———

The best way to learn Spirit-to-Spirit is to practice it. The following exercise is designed to help you do just that.

Exercise
-2-

Awakening Your Third Eye
THROUGH SPIRIT-TO-SPIRIT

There's no better way to become skilled at Spirit-to-Spirit than to use it for a great reason. In the following exercise you'll be activating your third eye, or sixth chakra, in order to make available (or *more* available) your classical clairvoyance. Remember, this is the type of sight that involves seeing colors and sometimes shapes and other images.

Because your imagination uses many of the same mechanics as does your psychic visioning, I'm going to put your imagination to use. We'll be visiting the Wizard of Oz to make this exercise accessible and enjoyable.

STEP ONE: **Perform Spirit-to-Spirit.** Acknowledge your personal spirit, the spirits of the spiritual beings helping with this process, and the Spirit.

STEP TWO: **Focus on Your Third Eye.** Bring your awareness to your third eye, or the sixth chakra, which is located between your eyes. Breathe deeply and ask the Spirit to activate this chakra so it can be used safely and wisely for your clairvoyant processes. Remain focused on your brow until you feel like the Spirit has cleaned and attuned this chakra.

STEP THREE: **Ask for Oz.** Request that the Spirit grant you an image of the Emerald City, which is resplendently green and shiny. Spend a few minutes exploring this magical city. Observe the various shades of green and other colors. Search for the City's dwellers, such as people, animals, and various magical beings. Then ask to psychically perceive the all powerful Oz. What does he look like? Know that as you focus on the Wizard, the Spirit is attuning your sixth chakra.

STEP FOUR: **Close.** Once you feel complete with the process, take a few deep breaths and ask the Spirit to return you to your everyday life.

————

Accept whatever you viewed. Next you'll learn about one of the most important concepts involved in clairvoyance—boundaries.

Subtle Boundaries

A Clairvoyant's Protection

Subtle energy boundaries are psychic parameters that filter incoming and outgoing information, both subtle and physical. The most important boundaries are your auric fields, which we discussed in the last chapter. Each layer acts like a filter for its related chakra. Because of this, clairvoyant success is dependent on having proper energetic boundaries—not only in relationship with your sixth chakra, but with any of the chakras you are going to interconnect with while pursuing or interpreting a clairvoyant vision.

What happens if your boundaries are too thin? You could become easily overwhelmed by visions or other mystical information. You can easily take in inapplicable or even harmful data. As a case in point, I once worked with a man named Jason who was devastated by his clairvoyant gift. He yearned to totally shut it down. From a young age he had received premonitions of horrifying situations in his nightly dreams. Most visions came true, and he hadn't been able to prevent any of them. As you might suspect, he struggled with insomnia.

During our time together, I helped Jason switch off the negative futuring and open to only positive and uplifting dreams. We used Spirit-to-Spirit and the technique featured next, Healing Streams of Grace, to accomplish this goal. It worked. His insomnia disappeared.

Yet another client was consistently awash with others' feelings, as well as images that illuminated the causes of their emotions. She was constantly on edge and felt guilty for "psychically spying," even though she wasn't trying to peer into others' lives. We used the Establishing Energetic Boundaries exercise, which you'll be shown in this chapter. This process enabled her to separate herself from others. As a result, her clairvoyance began to inspire her with visions that helped herself rather than intruded on others.

What happens if your boundaries are too thick or impenetrable? You might not get any clairvoyant images. One of my friends was frustrated because no matter what he did, he never received a vision. After conducting the Establishing Energetic Boundaries exercise on page 55, he started to dream in color. After a while, he then began receiving visions when meditating. The clairvoyant images increased in frequency over time. His boundaries needed to loosen up, whereas Jason's needed to shift.

Adjoining Spirit-to-Spirit with Healing Streams of Grace enables healthy boundaries and clairvoyant empowerment, as you'll soon see.

Technique Two

HEALING STREAMS OF GRACE

Healing Streams of Grace is a cornerstone process for interacting clairvoyantly. The foundation of this process is the recognition that the Spirit emanates endless waves of grace. I define grace as love that empowers positive change.

The easiest way to understand the healing streams of grace—which I'll also refer to as "the streams," "healing streams," or "streams of grace"—is as beams of light shining from the sun. The sun is the Spirit, and the arms of light, or healing streams of grace, are extensions of the Spirit's love. These streams are constantly available in whatever form is required. If there is a need, the stream is delivered and will remain attached as long as it is beneficial.

How and why might you call upon the healing streams? Imagine that you wake in terror because you dreamed that a friend is going to be stricken ill. What would you do? My suggestion would be to immediately conduct Spirit-to-Spirit. Once connected with the Spirit, ask that it send healing streams to your friend. The required streams will be brought to your friend and remain as long as needed. You can also ask for streams to help you return to sleep.

Healing streams can remove blocks to receiving visions, transform different chakric energies into a picture, erase a negative vision, write words under an image, or serve as your response to a vision. You'll be shown these and the dozens of important applications of the healing streams in chapters 3 through 8.

Want to use the healing streams for an important purpose? The following exercise will help you experiment with Spirit-to-Spirit and Healing Streams of Grace while establishing much-needed energetic boundaries.

Establishing Energetic Boundaries

This exercise will give you a quick way to cleanse and create subtle energy boundaries so that your auric field can act like a proper energetic filter. After walking through the steps enabling this protective measure, you'll practice your sixth chakra visualization.

STEP ONE: **Perform Spirit-to-Spirit.** Affirm your personal spirit, others' spirits, and the Spirit.

STEP TWO: **Make Your Request.** Ask the Spirit to send streams of grace through your auric field to cleanse and clean it. Know that these streams will remain connected to the individual fields that require additional purification or bolstering. Visualize beams of light flowing through your energy field and feel the resulting effects.

Now ask the Spirit to heal your field and show you what it's doing while performing this task. Through your sixth chakra, psychically perceive the colors or shapes of the streams that are filling in any energetic holes or leaks. Watch as the streams knit together any gaping areas, even out blotchy areas, and execute any other needed maneuvers.

STEP THREE: **Close.** As soon as your surrounding boundaries appear strong and you feel safe, ask to perceive the color or colors that represent your personal spirit. In chapter 3 you'll learn about the meaning of these colors. Right now, trust your sense of the colors that reflect you.

Watch as these signature colors emanate from your center like a beautiful fog that spreads throughout every corner of your being. These clouds of colors fill your auric field, assuring that you'll only attract energies that support your signature self. Under pressure, you can always visualize these colors dispersing throughout your being, supporting wholeness and well-being.

Take a few deep breaths and return to your everyday state.

———

Now that you've experienced the ease with which you can purify and establish your boundaries—and also vitalize your true self—you are ready to learn about a few more vital clairvoyant matters.

An Eye for Discernment

WHAT'S INVOLVED IN CLAIRVOYANCE?

One of the most fun (and challenging) truths about clair-voyance is that it is a multi-layered process. There are literally dozens of factors involved in receiving, interpret-ing, or sending a visual. A single vision, whether it's first recognized as a psychic vision, a feeling, a dream, or an environmental sign, is like a poem. You can analyze it for surface value alone. Then again, you can plummet its depths, unlocking complexities as you excavate.

How do you accomplish a multifaceted analysis? The following example is based on an image I received when shopping.

I was aimlessly roaming around a grocery store when I inadvertently wondered what might happen that evening. I hadn't performed Spirit-to-Spirit; I was simply musing. A picture popped into my mind of a happy little puppy wagging its tail.

Oh no, I thought. Was I about to inherit a stray dog? Or was the picture about my current huge companions? Although they are ninety pounds, each of my two dogs still acts like a puppy. In fact, Lucky, the yellow lab, will plop himself atop people as if he still weighs ten pounds. Then again, the picture could mean almost anything, maybe even represent a psychological issue. Perhaps I needed more play?

As this example reveals, a picture can take you in many different directions. Most of the time you have to dig to get to the meaning of an image. This is what I call "qualifying a vision." Quite literally, you must examine the qualifiers, or factors, that compose a vision.

When you receive an image of any sort—psychically or environmentally—there are a number of factors you want to assess. As I describe each qualifier, think about how you might better develop your own "eye for discernment" in regard to clairvoyance. Along the way, I'll keep returning to the puppy picture to explain the factors I'm describing. (And don't worry. After using this example to make my points, I'll tell you what the image really meant. You just have to wait until the end of the section.)

Voluntary or Involuntary Visions

Voluntary visions are those that you actively seek; involuntary ones come unbidden. The picture I received in the grocery store was involuntary, as I hadn't been requesting it. The most common processes used to cultivate a vision include meditation, prayer, interactions with another person or spiritual guides, and even drawing. Most of this book is devoted to showing you how to actively formulate or obtain a vision. However, you'll be shown how to analyze involuntary visions as well, although basically this is done in the same way as a vision received voluntarily.

Prescriptive or Descriptive Visions

Prescriptive visions reveal what must be done to make a correct decision. These visions might also suggest what could occur if we do "X" rather than "Y." Because of the futuristic twist to these images, we'll more thoroughly examine how to work with them in chapter 7. We'll also nominally cover this topic in chapter 4, in which we discuss prophetic visions, which are frequently prescriptive.

Descriptive images share information about attitudes, values, potentials, history, and facts. They provide data and insight. For instance, imagine that you are talking to a friend who is smiling but you sense that something isn't right. Perhaps you walk through Spirit-to-Spirit and get a psychic image of her crying. You can adjust your attitude accordingly.

Sometimes you can't tell if an image is prescriptive or descriptive. Was the picture of the puppy prescriptive? If so, I might have been getting a warning. Perhaps my son was going to bring home a new furry guest. Or was the image descriptive? In this case, the vision might have been indicating something needed by my current companions. The fun part of clairvoyance is that you always get to ask questions and obtain more visions to figure out matters like these.

Visions or Fantasies

When the puppy picture rolled into my mind's eye, the first query I should have made, after conducting Spirit-to-Spirit, was this: "Is this a fantasy or a real vision?" We can absorb fantasies from others—people, natural beings, or spirits—or make them up ourselves. There is no substance to a fantasy; therefore, we don't want to pay attention to them. Visions, however, aren't concocted. They are messages, and as such they are worth analyzing. The tell-tale difference between the two is that we can change or distort fantasies with our imagination, but we can't alter an actual clairvoyant image. We can obtain additional visions, but we can't reform a true vision.

Back to the grocery store. If I were on top of my clairvoyance, I might have tried to turn the pictured puppy into something else, maybe a horse or a dragon. If I could have modified the puppy, the image was probably a fantasy, my own or someone else's. But if the puppy image remained the same, then it would qualify as a true vision worth deciphering.

Literal or Figurative

An image might be literal, metaphorical, or a mix of both. Perhaps the puppy image was literal. In this case, it might have represented one of my true-life dogs or an incoming visitor. The picture could have been metaphorical, however. As such, it could have depicted an aspect of myself or of one of my dogs. Then again, the picture might have been both literal and metaphorical. Maybe it was showing a "literal Lucky" at an earlier age and metaphorically inferring that his inner nature hasn't changed.

It's critical to distinguish between realistic and metaphorical images, especially in relation to characters in an image. As an example, I was conducting a session for a client and saw a psychic picture of my father walking around. My father is deceased; however, my father literally could have showed up as a guide to give insight to my client. However, the image of my father also could have been a metaphor, stirring the client into thinking about their own father. When practicing your clairvoyance in this book, you'll be encouraged to ask your own spirit, the guides, or the Spirit if an image is literal or metaphoric. The answer might come via additional images or through other means, such as a verbal or empathic response, as well as by using other techniques. These processes will be taught to you in this book.

Sourcing

Sourcing is a verb that refers to identifying the source of a vision. It's vital to know if a vision comes from a trustworthy rather than an untrustworthy source. Basically, you want to pay attention to those which are divinely inspired and ignore the ones that aren't divinely approved. For instance, the puppy image might have been sent by the Spirit—or maybe by a negative entity that wanted to scare me into thinking I have three more years of raising a new puppy. Then again, I could have picked up on someone else's psychic radio frequency; perhaps a little first grader in the store was fantasizing about getting a puppy.

There are near-infinite numbers of sources. In a nutshell, the two fundamental source categories are the following:

WORLDLY OR OTHERWORLDLY: Worldly sources include living people, animals, plants, or other natural beings, and also aspects of yourself or others, such as an inner child or part of the soul. Otherworldly sources include the deceased, spiritual guides, masters, ghosts, angels, or interfering or negative entities or energies, which I often call "dark forces" or "interference." The basic difference is that worldly sources are alive, and otherworldly sources aren't clothed in flesh and blood.

SPIRIT-APPROVED OR NOT: Essentially, you only want to interface with sources of images and interpretative insights that are approved by the Spirit. The reason I use the Spirit-to-Spirit technique is to place the Spirit in charge of gathering the guidance allowed to create, interpret, or deliver an image. Know that it's never too late to conduct Spirit-to-Spirit. Perhaps you have a confusing dream one night. In the morning you can conduct Spirit-to-Spirit to request an interpretive vision.

Time Periods

An image can reflect any number of time periods. In fact, images sent in a sequence could each reflect a different time period. Because the time period noted will steer your analysis, you'll want to get clear about this matter.

There are three basic time periods that an image can portray. These are as follows:

BACK SIGHT: Also called hindsight, back sight
 visions are historical. They can show a situation
 that actually occurred in this life, a past life, or in
 between lives, but they may also indicate what
 could have happened if the storyline had played
 out differently.

CURRENT SIGHT: What is happening in the present? As upfront as this question might be,
 there are many types of current-day realities.
 A picture could connote your own or anyone
 else's present-day life as well as images from a
 parallel reality. Parallel realities are worlds that
 are co-created alongside this one. As an example, I once dreamed about a life I was living in
 a different plane of existence, although I was
 Cyndi on Earth. In the parallel life I was killed.
 As I clairvoyantly watched that parallel self shift

into my this-life self, I could feel that "other
Cyndi's" feelings and also gain her life's wisdom.

FUTURE SIGHT: Clairvoyance frequently offers
images of the future. The complication involves
figuring out if the provided image is a destiny
point (a certainty that will happen no matter
what), a probability (something that will most
likely occur), a possibility (an event that might
happen), or a warning (something that either
will, should, could, or shouldn't happen).
All these future-sight options and more are
addressed in chapter 7.

Additional Types of Sight

In addition to the types of sights listed above, there are
additional ones; several can apply to any time period.
They are as follows:

INSIGHT: Clairvoyant pictures don't always relate to
a time period. Sometime they contain advice or
wisdom that is universally applicable.

HALF SIGHT: Some images are partial, meaning that
they only reveal a small facet of a message. For
instance, I once received a half-sight image of a
man a client would meet. All I could see were

his shoes—they were hunting boots. My client was a corporate executive; the people in her life only wore dress shoes. When she met a man wearing hunting boots at a café, she was thrilled. Because of the half-sight image, she dated him. Now they are married. It wasn't important to see a full-sight picture, which I describe next. She only needed a clue to select her right mate.

FULL SIGHT: Pictures that reveal an overarching message are called full-sight visions. What's the difference between half-sight and full-sight pictures? Imagine that you ask for an image to show you what city to live in. You picture a city on a map in your mind's eye. This image is a full-sight image. Perhaps you next want to know which suburb—or block—would be best to search for a house. A half-sight image will serve as a telescope to zoom in on the answer.

———

One of the reasons that it's important to know about all the different types of sights is that you can take charge of the process. Imagine that you are trying to figure out the cause of a problem and you are shown your six-year-old self. However, you don't know the specific event. You can use Spirit-to-Spirit and request more data. There are any number of responses you might receive. A part of the first picture might become clearer, showing you the context of a positive or negative event. As well, your "telescopic vision" could zoom in on a clarifying aspect of the image or you could be shown a second image.

Okay, so what did the puppy image that I received in the grocery store end up meaning? I actually figured it out within a few minutes of seeing it. When standing near the cantaloupe stand, I ran through the possibilities I've covered in this chapter to date. I already knew I was working with an involuntary image, so I used Spirit-to-Spirit to figure out if the vision was literal or figurative. Basically, I tried to change the image of the puppy, but it held true. I was dealing with a real-life puppy.

Then I requested to know if the picture was prescriptive or descriptive. I saw words under the image (you'll learn how to access this tool in chapter 6). Based on what I read, I knew the vision related to the future.

The question still remained: Should I even pay attention to this picture? One way to respond to that query is to assess the source. In my head—no, I wouldn't be caught muttering to myself in a grocery store—I posed this question. I have a special way to verify that the source is the Spirit, using a tip I provided you earlier in this chapter. To me, the Spirit looks like a glowing golden light in the frame of an image. This light appeared next to the puppy. Okay, the puppy image came from the Spirit, or was at least Spirit-approved.

Finally, I used the technique "Expand the Image" on page 229 to obtain further information. The edges of the puppy picture seemed to expand. As the borders extended, I could see the puppy outside of the grocery store, near the exit. The exit and entrance are on different sides of the store. After purchasing my groceries, I walked outside. There was a stand with a woman and a puppy. The woman was fundraising for a dog shelter. I gave money, as that seemed to be what I was being divinely inspired to do.

Why did the Spirit even bother to provide a precursor image, since the fundraising stand and the puppy were already positioned outside of the store? Well, if anyone understands us, it's God. I'm constantly in a rush. Upon finishing my shopping, I probably would have run right by the fundraiser to accomplish my next task. The puppy image forced me to slow down and do the right thing.

There is yet another consideration to be aware of when qualifying or analyzing a vision. It's called point of view, and I'm covering this topic next. You'll actually get to practice the art of perceiving and changing points of view before the next chapter, just to get this activity under your belt.

Point of View

THE ROVING EYE

One of the most important considerations in clairvoyance involves distinguishing between points of view. Once you've figured out how to qualify a point of view, you can then change the point of view to obtain more precise or desirable information.

In a nutshell, point of view is the lens through which you observe a situation. Remember English class, when you were told to analyze literature via point of view? Well, that lesson is going to haunt you. The only difference between an author's point of view and a clairvoyant point of view is that *you* are the storyteller—or at least the story viewer interpreting the tale.

When perceiving a vision, your "eyes," whether inner or external, will see in one of four ways: first person, second person, third-person limited, or third-person omniscient. When experiencing a first-person vision, you are in a situation and watching it through your own eyes.

As such, you are the main interpreter of what is occurring. The benefit of first person is that you can figure out what the "you" in the vision thinks or feels. For instance, imagine that you are replaying an event that scared you when you were four years old. In a first-person vision you'll re-experience the situation as that four-year-old. In this way you can validate that self's experience and better address it when you return to your adult state.

When envisioning through the second-person point of view, your "physical" self is in a vision, but your "eyes" are outside of the vision, watching yourself. You're the observer of yourself, although you can also see what others are doing. For instance, let's say that you are trying to figure out if you want to travel with a new friend or not. You might psychically project into the future and observe how you will react to them when on vacation. You can use this analysis to make a smart decision. Basically, in a second-person vision you become an objective observer and can learn about yourself at a distance.

There are two third-person points of view. Third-person limited involves viewing all components of a psychic vision from a detached space, as if watching television. This point of view helps you perceive how everything and everyone fits together—including the self in a vision, if you are in it—from a surface perspective, like cogs and wheels. On the other hand, third-person omniscient is the God point of view. No matter who or what is featured in the vision, including yourself, you can dip into the minds, feelings, and souls of all involved. Third-person omniscient is an ideal point of view for gathering insights and understandings.

The table below will help you better comprehend the difference between the various points of view:

First Person	You are in the vision and watching everything and everyone through your own eyes.
Second Person	You are watching yourself while outside of yourself and are focused only on yourself, though others might be present.
Third-Person Limited	You are on the outside looking at what's occurring in the vision. You may or may not be in the vision.
Third-Person Omniscient	You are on the outside looking in, but you can see into and relate with everything and everyone. Omniscient allows you to fully comprehend the motives, feelings, beliefs, and needs of everyone and everything in a vision, including yourself, if you're in the vision.

Exercise
--5--

Changing Visual Points of View

In the following exercise, you will center in your sixth chakra while experiencing hindsight, the art of perceiving the past. In order to gain additional information about that historical moment, you'll also switch points of view.

PREPARE: Find a serene place in which to conduct this exercise.

STEP ONE: **Perform Spirit-to-Spirit.** Affirm your essential spirit, others' spirits, and the Spirit. Know that the Spirit will continually cleanse and sustain your subtle boundaries through- out this exercise, delivering streams of grace throughout all aspects of your being.

STEP TWO: **Center in Your Sixth Chakra.** Ask the Spirit to hold you within your sixth chakra. Now request that the Spirit assist you with activating and enabling your third-eye psychic activity while managing the ensuing process.

STEP THREE: **Select a Situation.** Choose a situation
from the past that you'd like to better understand. Select one that involves at least one other
person besides yourself.

STEP FOUR: **Relate Through First-Person Point of
View.** Review the situation as if living it again.
You will re-experience it through the body
you had at that time, seeing the event through
your long-ago eyes. Sense and feel how you are
reacting to this event.

STEP FIVE: **Relate Through Second-Person Point
of View.** Now exit your long-ago self and pretend to be a mouse in the corner. Watch how
the "you" in the situation is acting and interacting. What do your observations tell you about
yourself and the long-term effects the situation
has had on you?

STEP SIX: **Relate Through Third-Person Limited.**
Expand your viewfinder so you can assess the
entire situation as if you're watching television.
You aren't particularly aligned with any of the
characters, even the self from the past. What
does this surface review reveal about the situation—and yourself?

STEP SEVEN: **Relate Through Third-Person Omniscient.** It's time to "play God." You can view every character or part of the scene at will and also dive inside of all people, beings, or even objects in the situation. How does being omniscient help you comprehend the situation and how it has affected you?

STEP EIGHT: **Close.** Spend a few minutes reflecting on what you've learned. What perspectives did you gather from each point of view? What is your main takeaway? Is there any forgiveness work you need to do? If so, ask the Spirit to send streams of grace to all concerned parties. Then take a few deep breaths and return to your everyday awareness.

———

As you can see, my examples reveal several techniques for taking charge of your clairvoyant process. Succinctly, you can do the following, asking for your own spirits, others' spirits, or the Spirit to assist:

- analyze the first image
- ask for an additional image
- focus on a particular area
- zoom in and out of any part of a picture

- move around time periods
- alter points of view
- ASK QUESTIONS!

You'll learn even more about how to accomplish these tasks throughout this book. The reason that I've emphasized the last suggestion, however, is that I've discovered that one of the most important factors for receiving and comprehending visions is to know what questions to ask myself, the guides, or the Spirit. That's why I next offer a beginner's list of the types of questions I employ when I'm interacting clairvoyantly.

Questions for Assessing a Vision

The following questions sum up the points made in this chapter to provide you a "cheat sheet" of questions pertinent to obtaining or analyzing a clairvoyant image. In parentheses I've labeled the qualifier that the question relates to. You'll gather more questions as we move through this book. For instance, you'll add futuristic questions in chapter 7. I'll summarize all the points made so you have a complete list of questions in the appendix.

You'll be learning how to understand or interpret these questions using the techniques featured in chapters

3 through 8, though there are several ways that you'll receive answers to prompting queries. As I've already suggested, changes might appear on the original image. You might receive a second image. Two of your best interpretive tools, however, are your common sense and memories. If your initial impression implies a certain meaning, go for it. If a depiction has held a specific meaning to you across time, it still will, even in a clairvoyant image. And you'll need to trust your gut. If you ask a question such as, "Is this image literal or metaphorical?" (which is included in the following list), you might simply "know" the answer. As you play with these questions (starting on page 77) and those added to the collection throughout the book, you'll also develop your own interpretive style.

I especially like the last question on page 78. In fact, most of the questions I ask in my head for a client are sent to me by the Spirit or spiritual guides. After all, receiving a helpful answer is often dependent on asking the correct leading question.

———

Having covered the most significant factors related to psychic visioning, you are now ready to plunge into the most active form of clairvoyance: classical clairvoyance. And that's what you'll do in the next chapter.

* * * * *

"Cheat Sheet" Questions

- Is this vision one I wanted to receive or is it just popping in? (voluntary or involuntary)

- If this image is involuntarily received, should I use Spirit-to-Spirit to further analyze it or not?

- Is this an actual vision or a fantasy? (visions cannot be altered; fantasies can)

- Is this image literal or metaphorical? (literal versus figurative)

- Who or what is showing me these images? (sourcing)

- Is this a Spirit-approved source of images? (sourcing)

- Is there a more Spirit-approved source of images that can help me psychically? (sourcing)

- Can I see more of the image? (full sight)

- Can I hone in on the most vital part of the image? (half sight)

- Through what point of view am I perceiving this image? (first person, second person, third-person limited, third-person omniscient)

- Is there a better point of view for understanding this image? (first person, second person, third-person limited, third-person omniscient)

- Is this image revealing an important idea? (insight)

- Is this picture about right now? (current sight)

- Is this vision about the past? (back sight/hindsight)

- Is this vision about the future? (foresight; further questions related to futuring are included in chapter 7)

- Is this vision related to the future or right now? (prescriptive or descriptive; prescriptive visions are more thoroughly discussed in chapters 4 and 7)

- Can I receive another image to help interpret this one?

- Am I supposed to take an action based on this image?

- Is someone else supposed to take an action based on this insight?

- If this image relates to someone else, should I mention it? If so, how?

- Can I receive more information to clarify the following? (characters—people, beings, objects, props, etc.—interactions, time period, interpretations of elements)

- Can I be shown or told what other questions I should ask?

• • • • • • •

Summary

There are two main techniques you can use when receiving, interpreting, or sending a psychic vision: Spirit-to-Spirit and Healing Streams of Grace. These processes will assist you in qualifying a vision, or assessing the components to arrive at the correct interpretation. They can also help you establish subtle-energy boundaries (the protection needed to operate safely while being clairvoyant) and become actively involved in a visual process.

As per the qualifiers, after figuring out if you received a voluntary or involuntary vision, you can then assess for several other factors. These include identifying if a vision is prescriptive, descriptive, or both; fantasy or true; and literal or figurative. You can also evaluate for the source, time period, and type of a vision, such as insight, half sight, or full sight. Another important factor is checking for point of view. The upside of understanding the various points of view is that you can interpret a vision knowing what view you are using but also alter the viewpoint, thus gaining an additional perspective.

One of the tricks in clairvoyant analysis is to know what questions to ask to prompt further visioning, which is why you've been presented with a cheat sheet at the end of this chapter. We'll add to this list as we go.

• • • •

CHAPTER THREE

Classic Clairvoyance
SEEING THE SIGHTS
THROUGH YOUR
THIRD EYE

Seers, oracles, diviners, intuitives, shamans—these and other types of mystics commonly employ classical clairvoyance, which involves using the third eye, or sixth chakra, for psychic visioning.

Classical clairvoyance is the backbone of clairvoyance. Classical visions are those that appear in a variety of colors, shapes, and forms. They stream through our mind as photos or movies. They can materialize on a mind screen or be spied through the physical eyes. These are the images that people "ooh" and "ahh" over. These are the splendid visions that inform, instruct, and explain.

In the last chapter you experienced Spirit-to-Spirit and Healing Streams of Grace, techniques you'll use throughout the remainder of this book. You also practiced establishing subtle boundaries and distinguishing between several other important interpretative qualifiers or factors. You'll add to this toolkit in this chapter with information specific to the interpretation of classical visions. The tips provided include assessing for colors, energetic attachments, shapes and symbols, and location, as well the use of a variety of focusing tools such as foodstuffs, stones, and oils.

Then we'll put this newfound knowledge (and last chapter's insights) to work. I'll more thoroughly explain each of the three types of classical clairvoyance: inner visions, external visions, and dreams, the categories first introduced in chapter 1. I'll then present you with exercises for each of the three areas. In keeping with our goal of building a full-out set of questions to ask when being clairvoyant, I'll end this chapter with a few additional questions to add to the list started in chapter 2.

Know that you'll employ the information in this chapter in chapters 4 through 8, which showcase additional ways to apply classical clairvoyance, as well as prophetic visioning, which is explained in the next chapter. Enjoy this entrée into the world of wonder that has occupied mystics across time.

Important Tips and Tools

FOR CLASSICAL CLAIRVOYANCE

There are dozens of factors explaining the meaning of a classical clairvoyant image. The main areas include color, energetic attachments, shapes and symbols, and location. There are also several focusing tools that can support the clairvoyant process. When analyzing factors like these, as well as those described in the last chapter, you might grasp the entire message in a single image.

That's not always true, however. The most successful clairvoyant is one who remains fluid with the process. Information is king, and you get more information by remaining in charge of your clairvoyant process. That's why, in this section, I will describe the main qualifiers and give you examples that explain their use. I'll offer questions that you can ask upon receiving a certain type of image that will prompt further insights. Keep this chapter handy; you can return to it to analyze any classical vision—and even some prophetic visions.

Analyzing for Color

Color is the keynote of the classical clairvoyant image. When classical pictures are formed within the sixth chakra—or are perceived through the everyday eyes—they appear in color.

What do the different colors indicate? How do you interpret "off" colorations, which might be murky or blotchy? Comprehending the basic meaning of the various colors and hues will help you interpret classical clairvoyant pictures.

For instance, imagine that you have sought a vision about how to respond to your mom, who seems "off." You conduct Spirit-to-Spirit and receive a psychic picture of your mother with red streaks of energy emanating from her. You also spy a murky gray blob inside of her heart. After examining the information about color meanings in this section, you discover that red can represent anger. But the gray? It's now obvious to you that your mother is hiding something important in her heart. This analysis can prompt you to ask loving questions to ferret out your mother's true feelings.

I'm now going to present two tables. The first indicates the meaning of the basic colors. The second describes the "off" hues. In this second category I also share a few questions that could prompt a deeper analysis of the hue discolorations.

COLOR	INDICATIONS
Red	Passion, vitality, energy, survival issues, basic physical health, pain or injury site, inflammation, anger
Orange	Emotions, creativity, sensuality, excitement
Yellow	Thoughts, facts, mentality, willpower; also issues related to success
Green	New energy and issues related to love, renewal, relationship
Blue	Communication, expression; a calming energy
Indigo	Strength and power; connection between what one thinks and does
Purple/violet	Royalty, clairvoyance, insight, strategy, predictions about the future
White	Purity, spirituality, purpose; also issues involving the Spirit
Black	Shamanic power, ability to manifest; can also indicate negativity or evil
Gray	Something is being hidden or covered up
Silver	Protective quality, deflects evil; can indicate information is being transmitted from the Spirit
Gold	Harmony; spiritual power that manifests what the Spirit desires
Brown/earth tones	Naturalness, groundedness, ancestry

• • • •

HUE	INDICATION
Murky	Something vital is hidden. Ask what needs to be uncovered.
Blotchy	The situation is cloudy and confusing. Ask what issues are being disguised.
Too light	The situation is missing a vital insight. Ask what needs to be known.
Too dark	Negativity is present. Ask what or who is interfering.
Leaking energy	Areas through which energy is being lost. In a clairvoyant image, leaks look like holes or depressed areas. Usually energy is emanating out of a chakra, auric field, or bodily site. Ask why there is a leak.

———

Keep in mind that it doesn't matter if you understand the first colors or hues that appear. You can always use Spirit-to-Spirit to ask for further clarification. Change points of view, request images from the past (or concurrent realities or the future) to elaborate; see if changing psychic sources will make a difference. Just ask!

For instance, imagine that you perceive energy leaking out of a friend's head when you are "checking in" for them. You might request to know what caused the problem. You might see a picture of a swing set. Desiring a further explanation, you request more data and obtain a second image of your friend as a small child falling off the swings and hitting her head. You want to know what problems this has caused and get a third image, that of red energy pounding in her head. Your friend confirms that sometimes she gets headaches. Three simple images have provided your friend a lot of information.

Analyzing for Energetic Attachments

Energetic attachments are unhealthy bonds. They can occur between individuals, a person and a group, people (or a person) and a living being such as an animal, and even people (or a person) and an object. No matter who or what these attachments connect, they are limiting. In fact, an attachment operates like a contract that decides what energy can be exchanged or not between the contractual members. While it might seem that one member of an attachment benefits more than another, that's never true. Everyone loses out.

For instance, imagine that a specific type of attachment called a "cord" exists between a mother and her child. In the scenario, the child is an accidental pregnancy. In order to assure that it is allowed into the developing body, the child's soul forges a contract with the maternal soul. The agreement is that the child will take on all the mother's issues, including her physical and emotional troubles, while the mother receives an extra dollop of the child's life energy, which emanates from the first chakra energy, in order to make it through the pregnancy. Attachments such as these don't disappear unless they are released consciously. This means that forever after, until dealt with by either party, the child will be stuck with the mother's challenging energy and also lack vital energy.

In this example, it might seem that the mother is prospering from the contract, but the truth is that both contract affiliates are suffering. Obviously, the child will be overly ill, emotional, and tired. But the mother will be prevented from dealing with her own issues. And aren't we here to face—and deal with—our own deficits and assets? The key to growth is self-honesty and responsibility.

As stated, energetic attachments can exist between almost anyone and anything. They can lock into a bodily area, a chakra, an auric field, or just about anything or anywhere else. Clairvoyance is a potent process for detecting and releasing these attachments. Following are ways to perceive attachments and tips for understanding the reasons one exists. You'll learn how to release attachments in chapter 8.

Ways to Perceive Attachments

CORDS: A cord is an unhealthy energetic attachment that psychically looks like a garden hose and connects two or more beings, compromising all. If you are affected by a cord, you will be losing energy to the other cord holder, receiving undesirable energy, or both. Ask to whom or what the cord is connected and how this cord is causing limitations.

CURSES: A curse is an energetic device that creates problems for the accursed. It psychically looks like a messy collection of cords. Ask what or who caused the curse and what the curse entails.

SLASHES: Slashes are injuries caused by someone or something else. In a clairvoyant image they look like knife wounds. Ask who or what is doing the slashing and why.

Analyzing for Shapes and Symbols

Shapes are symbols that convey an energetic meaning. There are several basic shapes, each of which steers energy toward a specific purpose. For instance, as you'll learn in the following outline of shapes and their meanings, squares are protective. Let's say that you receive a classical psychic image in which a dad is drawing a square shape around his child. You can assume that the dad plays a protective role in his child's life.

Numbers are also symbolic and hold meaning. It's smart to pay attention to how many objects, people, or other factors appear in a vision, or if a number itself is the subject of a vision. Regarding the latter, imagine that you've asked the question "How many times a day should I exercise?" If you see a "2" in your head, you've received a pretty clear answer.

The numbers of characters or objects that appear in a vision can also mean something. For instance, I once worked with a client who was raised with two siblings. Her mother came to the session with her. Even though my client—the daughter—kept telling me that she had two brothers, I kept seeing a third brother. The mother turned a bright purple and gasped. The mom shared that she had become pregnant as a teenager and given up the baby for adoption. That child had been a boy. My image was correct. Although the mother hadn't been prepared to deal with her history, she decided to do so in the wake of the session. She reached out to the adoption agency and ended up contacting the oldest son, who was happy to connect with his birth family. The hard news became good news.

The next two tables will help you work with shapes and numbers. In the first table I relay the various shapes and explain what they indicate. In the second table I'll explain numbers. Also provided are questions that you can use to more fully pinpoint the meaning of a clairvoyantly perceived shape or number.

SHAPE	INDICATION
Triangle	Creative. Something is being formed or created. Ask what must be understood to create something positive.
Square	Protective. Squares hold energy within them, keeping these energies safe. You can ask if more protection is needed, what energy is being protected within an envisioned square, and if this energy should be held within the square or not. For instance, you want to protect your inner child in a square but not enclose or bury someone else's energies, which will cause disturbance.
Circle	Relational. Represents relationships and connections. Ask what connections are formed by the circle and if they are healthy or not.
Spiral	Counterclockwise spirals take energy out, and clockwise spirals bring energy in. Ask what is being taken in or released and if what is happening is healthy or not.
Cross	The vertical line represents spiritual connection and the horizontal bar connects to the everyday world. For example, if someone has a cross in their fourth chakra, you'll check the vertical line to see who or what they are spiritually connected to and the horizontal line to see whom in the world they are bonded with.

NUMBER	INDICATION
1	Beginnings or do-overs. Ask what is starting up.
2	Partnership. Ask if the pairing is healthy or not.
3	Intelligence and productivity. Ask what is being formed.
4	Balance, fairness, healing. Ask if more balance is needed.
5	Communication and creation. Ask what the Spirit would like to communicate to bring about a change.
6	Mystical traveling, strategy, the future. Ask what choices are involved in opening to a spiritual message or creating a better future.
7	Spiritual empathy, prophecy, purpose. Ask the Spirit to provide guidance about whatever is occurring.
8	Karma, timelessness, joining of feminine and masculine traits. Ask the Spirit how to release karma preventing magical events and clear perceptions.
9	Completion, success, earthly mastery. Ask what will bring projects and desires fully into the material reality.

For double-digit numbers, add the two numbers and look up the single digit result on this chart. For instance, a 10 reduces to a 1 plus 0, which is 1.

• • • •

Use logic to interpret images that are broken, mis-shapen, incomplete, or distorted. If you see a symbol that seems "off," you can ask what is causing a problem and what can be done to fix it. For instance, let's say that you perceive a crooked square around someone's energy field. You can surmise that this person lacks sufficient protection. Knowing this, you can ask the Spirit more direct questions about the issues involved, and then go about using Spirit-to-Spirit and applying healing streams to fix matters. If you see a crooked "2," you might ask what is causing a broken partnership. Keep asking for additional images, change the point of view, or take another tack to better understand what has appeared.

The Meaning of Location

The locations shown in a vision can clue you in on the image's meaning. There are two types of locations. The first is the landscape or backdrop featured in a vision. In general, this part of a vision is environmental in nature, most usually the scenery around the central figure. When assessing a landscape, you might also focus on a vital part of the scenery or a featured activity. The second aspect of location relates to the focal points on the vision's character/s, such as a bright color emphasizing a person or animal's chakra or body part.

In regard to a landscape, your favored interpretive tool should be common sense. For instance, if you intuitively perceive yourself in a tent in the forest, you'll probably guess that you might enjoy camping. Landscape images, however, might be metaphorical or realistic. For instance, let's say you are wondering if you should get romantically involved with a person you recently met. After conducting Spirit-to-Spirit, you psychically envision a desert.

Does the desert indicate that there isn't anything for you in the relationship? If so, the image is metaphorical. But maybe the vision is suggesting that you travel to the desert with your newfound love. In this case, the image is realistic. You'll want to ask the Spirit to give you an additional image to better define the original picture.

Also pay attention to the focus of a picture. If a person or object is being highlighted, that's where you'll perform an assessment. For instance, let's say that you perceive an image of a huge crowd, and a spotlight shines on one particular person. You'll now request additional knowledge about that person. But if the brightest figure in the landscape is a tree, you'll be working to interpret what message is being conveyed by that tree.

The second type of location that can emerge in a clairvoyant process is bodily or energetic, such as related to a specific chakra or auric field. Every bodily area reflects a certain meaning; so does each chakra and auric field. As a case in point, imagine that your stomach hurts. You attune and receive a psychic image of your abdomen. On the left side of the abdomen is a big red circle.

What have we already learned in this chapter? Red relates to passion or inflammation. A circle indicates relationship. We also know from chapter 1 that the abdomen is the home of the second chakra, which regulates feelings. A short section provided on page 99 about chakras and their meanings will reiterate this point.

In the first outline associated with this section, you'll learn that the small intestine sorts what's useful from what's not; also, that the left side of the body is feminine in nature. Putting all factors together, you might guess that your pain could be caused by a relationship (the circle) in which you are receiving (left side) unhealthy emotional information (second chakra, small intestine) and are angry (red) about it.

The next two tables will help you understand the meaning of specific body parts and chakras. In the Body Part table I describe the types of energies managed by specific body parts as well as areas of the body—right versus left, and also top, middle, and bottom. The second table will refresh your knowledge of the chakras and what each one manages. The meaning of the various auric fields will correspond to their related chakras.

BODY PART	INDICATION
Right side of body	Runs masculine concerns; indicates actions to take
Left side of body	Regulates feminine concerns, such as letting in goodness and love
Top third of body	Reflects spiritual beliefs and needs
Middle third of body	Governs thoughts, feelings, and everyday interactions
Bottom third of body	Manages physical needs; reflects historical issues
Under the feet	Connects the body to its ancestry and the earth
Feet	Regulates movements forward
Knees	Establishes direction to take
Thighs	Holds parental issues
Hips	Provides energy for action
Intestines, Small	Sorts through nourishment and information— what's useful or not
Intestines, Large	Releases waste
Liver	Governs masculine power
Gallbladder	Reflects dreams and goals

Pancreas	Determines one's receptivity to life's sweetness
Stomach	Processes raw nourishment and incoming data
Spleen	Controls feminine power
Heart	Presides over one's ability to love; holds heart's desires
Shoulders	Stores issues for the heart; empowers decisions
Elbows	Makes space for one's self
Hands	Determines what someone is willing to give and take
Lungs	Reflects self-worth and grief issues
Ribs	Protects the heart and self-interest
Neck	Invites the expression and receiving of information
Face	Shows the world what one wants it to see
Cranium	Regulates the connection to the earth and the heavens
Ears	Monitors what someone will listen to or not
Eyes	Decides what someone will see or not see

CHAKRA/FIELD	INDICATION
First	Security, safety, physical health, passion
Second	Feelings, creativity
Third	Thoughts, beliefs, work success, structure
Fourth	Love, healing, relationships
Fifth	Communication, philosophy; what is heard or not
Sixth	Strategy, self-image, the future
Seventh	Spirituality, purpose

One of the most illuminating activities is to work with locations in an image. For instance, let's say that I asked the Spirit to help me select which movie to see on a Friday evening. In response, I'm provided an image of myself sitting in a theater. My face looks happy—but I don't know which movie I'm watching. By shifting to third-person limited, I can glance at the screen and see the movie; now I know the best one to see. Let's also say that I don't know who I should ask to accompany me. I can now zoom into the original image and look at the seats next to me. There's my best friend!

What else can I do with my knowledge of bodily and energetic locations? Perhaps I don't know what the weather will be like when I exit the theater. Still interacting with the primary picture, I can focus on my upper body. I'm wearing a jacket. Now I know it's going to be cold out, so I should dress accordingly.

As silly as the example I just provided might be, think about how beneficial this flexibility could be if you are deciding to undergo chemotherapy, marry a particular person, or take a new job. I've found it critical to remember that, with the Spirit's help, I can delve and dive for information. After all, I'm using my own energetic gift.

Focusing Tools for Classical Clairvoyance

Across times, clairvoyants have used dozens—if not hundreds—of tools to help them receive and better interpret a clairvoyant image. Focusing tools can perform any number of tasks. Some calm and soothe the body, making it easier to meditate or pray. Others energize the system, rousing the clairvoyant energy. Yet other tools can compel spirits or the Spirit to assist with the receiving, interpretation, or sending of a vision.

The three main areas we'll briefly address in this section involve the use of specific foods, stones, and similar objects for clairvoyant conduction. This is not an exhaustive outline; there are many books and websites that provide insight and advice. I've shared just enough to get you going.

Foods for Clairvoyance

Nearly every culture I've studied or visited suggests certain foodstuffs to either improve one's clairvoyant activity or decrease resistance to the same. Classical clairvoyance, which involves the sixth chakra, is no exception. Following are a few recommendations:

EAT CHOCOLATE: Really! One of my first teachers explained that chocolate in its most raw state—or cocoa—can help someone ground but also expand clairvoyantly. When grounded, our energetic boundaries will be strong and keep us safe. Under these conditions, we'll feel safe when opening to clairvoyant images. I suggest using organic dark chocolate.

GO FOR FRUITS AND VEGETABLES: Cleansing foods purify the body and your chakras, inviting clearer and stronger images.

ELIMINATE UNHEALTHY FOODS: Heavy-duty gluten products, as well as cow's milk and chemically laden foods, make your body sluggish. In turn, your clairvoyant mechanisms will operate slowly.

SELECT POTENT SPICES AND HERBS: Anise is
known for increasing clairvoyance, as is lemon.
Bay is protective, and cinnamon raises your
vibration. Eyebright is said to help you see
fairies, and lemongrass is a great overall tonic for
enabling intuition. Marigold tea is also said to
enhance visions.

DRINK WATER: Drink plenty of water. Intuition
involves the flow of psychic and physical energy,
and water keeps our body's energy moving.

Stones and Objects for Clairvoyance

Various crystals, gemstones, and rocks can be used to
enhance our subtle boundaries, activate the third eye,
enhance the quality of clairvoyant images, and, as you'll
learn in chapter 8, send pictures and messages to others.
Certain objects have been used in hundreds of cultures
across time to create clairvoyant focus. The stones and
objects in my clairvoyant medicine bag include the following:

VIOLET AND INDIGO (BLUISH-PURPLE) COLORED
STONES: These will develop and bolster your
classical clairvoyant potential, as they relate to
the chakras involved in the activity. Amethyst

is protective and attunes the third eye; azurite enables past-life recall and dreaming; purple fluorite is protective and enhances visions; and iolite activates the third eye. You can hold one of these stones or gaze into them when interacting clairvoyantly. As well, lapis lazuli supports nighttime dreaming when put under the pillow.

CLEAR STONES: Quartz crystal will clear negative energy, attract angels and positive guides, and clarify vital messages. Consider using a clear quartz crystal ball as a focus point for generating images. Activate your third eye by staring into the ball while conducting Spirit-to-Spirit. You won't necessarily see an image in the crystal ball, but your inner images will be brighter.

PINK QUARTZ: Pink quartz represents love and always brings about the highest desires and visions.

RIVER ROCKS: Rocks indigenous to water, and even shells, will keep your emotions flowing and also release emotions that could interfere with clairvoyant activity.

ROCKS: Regular rocks—yup, like the kind found
on the ground, on a mountain, or even in your
landscaping—are very grounding. Consider
setting a few rocks near your feet to keep you
grounded while operating clairvoyantly.

WANDS: Crystal wands of any color can be used to
focus healing streams of grace. You can hold
the end and point the tip toward a part of your
body or someone else's body at the site requir-
ing assistance. Then psychically view the color
or streams of light pouring through the wand
into the needy area. You can also draw a picture
of your own or another's problem, conduct
Spirit-to-Spirit, and ask that the Spirit deliver
needed energy through the wand directly into
the challenged area. You can even point a
crystal wand at a medical scan and ask for the
delivery of grace.

MIRRORS AND WATER: Since ancient times diviners have stared into a mirror or a pool of water
in order to attune clairvoyantly. You may or
may not perceive an actual image in the mirror
or water, but the activity turns off the logical
brain and activates the intuitive brain, thereby
enhancing clairvoyance.

Essential Oils for Clairvoyance

Essential oils can greatly enhance your psychic capabilities. You can apply an oil to the third-eye area, use a diffuser, or drip oil on a candle. (Use caution: oils can be flammable!) Well-known clairvoyance-enhancing oils are:

BASIL: Clears negativity and helps with divination and clairvoyance.

FENNEL: Deflects negative entities and energies and protects from black magic.

FRANKINCENSE: Activates meditative states and invites connection to spiritual guides.

JASMINE: Enables dream recall and enhances the third eye.

LAVENDER: Calms, soothes, and protects.

MUGWORT: Promotes visions. Can be irritating, so be cautious.

MYRRH: Cleans the energy field, attracts blessings, and purifies.

PEPPERMINT: Promotes dreams and glimpses into the future.

SAGE: Cleans and strengthens spiritual energy; can also be burned as a sage stick.

SANDALWOOD: Cleans and purifies, releasing the past.

Are you ready to put all this information to work? Let's do so within three main areas of classical clairvoyance.

In the next three sections, I'm going to describe the three main types of classical visions, which were first introduced in chapter 1. As a reminder, these are internal, external, and dream-based visions. Most exciting, I'll outline exercises to employ within these areas. These exercises will draw on the interpretive qualifiers shared in chapter 2 and within this chapter.

Classical Clairvoyance
INNER VISIONS

Inner visions appear on the internal mindscape. These are the visions that I receive most frequently when I'm working. I'll give you an example.

During one session, I first psychically perceived my client dressed in a white shirt. Because I conduct Spirit-to-Spirit before opening to visions, I was already connected to the Spirit and the spiritual guides, so I set about qualifying the vision.

Right away, I wanted to know if the vision was prescriptive or descriptive, but the image didn't change, nor did I get a second picture. This told me that I wasn't going to be told or that the issue wasn't important. When you don't get a response, you move on. So then I asked (silently) if the shirt was literal or figurative. I had no idea what my client did for a living. Maybe he wore a lab coat in his job? The image of the shirt began to glow. Because the shirt didn't look concrete anymore, I knew that I was dealing with a metaphor.

I asked the Spirit to better explain the image, and instantly a bright white light appeared over the client's heart area. The heart represents love, and white indicates purity and spiritual purpose. At this point, I knew enough to inform my client that his deepest yearning was to serve the Spirit and help others do the same. He was a mechanic but told me that this assessment was accurate.

The next series of visions unfolded quickly. One image featured my client selling cars. In another, I saw him entering a school and paying cash to a bursar. Upon hearing about these images, my client became teary. Indeed, he had been buying and fixing cars as a side business, hoping to save enough money to attend ministerial school. At the end of the session, because of the few simple visions that the Spirit sent the client, he decided to really commit to his dream.

This story illustrates one of several common clairvoyant scenarios. In the case just shared, I didn't understand the visions, but the client did. Sometimes the reverse is true. Other times, neither of us know what's going on. I've learned, however, that most real (versus fantasy) visions make sense over time.

For example, during one session, I saw the psychic image of a farm. My female client was baffled, as was I. She was an accountant with no affiliation with farming. I told her to go about her life and set the vision aside. Maybe it would mean something later or even help her make a decision down the road. Within a year, she met a farmer, and they started dating. She was only open to dating him because of the psychic image she'd been provided.

Sometimes images are confusing because the picture is meant for someone besides the image's recipient. For example, I once perceived a psychic image of a tutu for a corporate officer in a Fortune 500 company. He didn't relate. Later, his wife came to see me. She shared that the day I'd received the tutu image, their young daughter had asked if she could take dance lessons. Because of the image granted the husband, the wife put their daughter in ballet classes.

Sometimes a client actually understands an image but pretends not to. (We might do the same with images we receive for ourselves.) With one client, the first picture I saw was of a bottle of vodka. She grew angry and said that the picture made no sense. Her life partner came to see me months later. Guess what the life partner discussed? Her mate's alcoholism.

There are so many ways to interpret a psychic vision that I want to give you my best advice: ask questions! Use Spirit-to-Spirit and take your time with a psychic vision. Don't jump to conclusions, but don't be scared to analyze a vision either. If you are meant to understand the meaning of an image, you eventually will.

Want to know how to summon a classical clairvoyant image? The next exercise will help you do exactly that.

Exercise
--6--

Classical Sixth Chakra Visioning

In the last chapter you awakened your sixth chakra through the Awakening Your Third Eye Through Spirit-to-Spirit exercise. Now you'll consciously cultivate a psychic vision and work toward comprehending it.

This exercise involves starting from scratch to ask for a psychic vision from the Spirit. It will be open-ended, meaning that you'll rely on the Spirit to select the topic. Feel free to use a special oil or gemstone when conducting the exercise—or perhaps you'll want to grab a bite of chocolate first.

PREPARE: Find a comfortable and quiet spot in which to meditate. Take a few deep breaths and relax your body.

STEP ONE: **Conduct Spirit-to-Spirit**. Affirm your own essence, that of the spirits that are assisting, and the Spirit. Bring your focus to your third-eye area and ask that the Spirit give you a meaningful image. If you want, you can picture a blank white screen in your mind's eye and watch a vision form upon it.

STEP TWO: **Concentrate on the Image.** Allow the image to come into focus. Trust whatever you perceive. Now begin to analyze this image based on what you've learned so far in this book. You'll get additional images in response to these questions:

- What is the source?

- Is this a real vision or a fantasy?

- Is this vision literal or metaphorical?

- What sight is involved in this image? (full sight, half sight, hindsight, current sight, foresight, insight)

- Would it be better to perceive this image through another type of sight? (same list as above)

- What is the current point of view? (first person, second person, third-person limited, third-person omniscient)

- Would a different point of view provide more information? (same list as above)

- Is this vision prescriptive or descriptive?

- What does the above—prescriptive or descriptive—tell me about the vision's meaning?

- What do I need to know about the source of this image?

- What data is provided me in terms of the following factors: colors (clear colorations, "off" colorations), attachments such as cords or curses, shapes and symbols, characters (who or what appears in the vision), interactions or events, locations (landscapes, bodily, chakra/field, or any others that stand out), time period/era, or any other factors?

Now ask the following questions:

- Can I receive another image to help interpret this one?

- Am I supposed to take an action based on any or all images?

- Can I be shown or told what other questions I should ask?

STEP THREE: **Request Healing Streams of Grace.** Is there a need to request healing streams for yourself or anyone else? Ask the Spirit to deliver the needed streams.

STEP FOUR: **Close.** Remain focused on the original or a vital follow-up picture until you feel clear about the Spirit's message. Then take a few deep breaths, thank the Spirit, and return to your everyday life when ready.

Additional Tip

Visioning for Others

What if you are conducting the previous exercise for someone else? I do this constantly through my client work.

Your basic approach remains the same. You simply ask the Spirit for an image on behalf of the other person or even for a group. As you're analyzing the image, you'll need to decide how—or if—to share it. You can use the following questions to receive images that will help you make this determination:

- Should I share the image or not?
- Is it appropriate to present my perspective or not?
- Is there an additional image that will assist the other?
- Should I request healing streams for myself, the other person, or anyone else involved in this interaction?

How might responses to these questions appear? I usually receive an additional clue on the original image or a new image. For instance, when asking "Should I communicate my perspective with a client or not?" I might get a big red X on my image if the response is a no. If it's appropriate to share, I might get a big sunny smile imprinted on the picture.

Remember to pay attention to the source of the image. When interacting with another person, I frequently end up communicating with *their* spiritual guides, not my own. After all, their personal guides know them better than mine do! Sometimes I get a picture of their information sources, such as an image of a deceased ancestor or angel. If this happens, I ask the Spirit if it's appropriate to share my insights about who or what is sourcing with my client.

Exercise
--7--

Reading Another's Auric Field

One of the most metaphysical activities involves reading the auric field. As explained in chapter 1, each auric field is partnered with a chakra. One layer, or field, lies atop another to form the overall auric field, which extends beyond the body.

Across time, clairvoyants have examined the colors, shapes, hues, extension, and relative brightness versus dullness of an individual's auric field to perceive what is occurring in the client's life. Images can consist of psychic impressions or be seen with the eyes. An assessment might involve assessing a single field, multiple fields, or the overall field. Here I'm going to give you a few tips for working clairvoyantly with someone else's field.

If you want to perceive another's field with your eyes, place your subject, seated or standing, next to a white or tan wall. If possible, turn on a nearby lamp; the reflection will help you see their aura. Then position yourself about ten feet away from your subject and gaze into the space around their body. It's easiest to perceive energy around the head, shoulder, and chest areas, which emanate strong electromagnetic activity.

If you are able, gauge the light or corona generated from the subject's body. If nothing appears, squint and try again. If the process doesn't work, evaluate for psychic images using the tips provided later in this section. If you do perceive an energy, determine the overall brightness and extension of their light. In general, the brighter the light, the happier and healthier the subject in that moment. The more extended the emanation, the more secure the person feels.

There are many ways that the aura might appear. You could perceive a single line of color threading through the greater aura. The specific auric fields are the same colors as their partnered chakras. You can evaluate this band of energy for color and hue, blotchiness, shapes, cords, and more. If you see a few colors flowing around the person, you are perceiving several fields at once and can analyze with the techniques you've already been taught. Are there holes? "Off" hues? Cords? Most usually, my students perceive a sort of white glow surrounding the subject. This image portrays the seventh auric field, which is the most spiritual. Know that whatever you see, when the person's life or mood shifts, so might their aura. An auric reading can only spot tendencies and take a Polaroid of a moment in time.

Most of us have greater luck examining another's auric field with psychic visioning techniques. The following exercise will help you conduct a psychic aura reading if you are interacting in person or on the phone.

PREPARE: Make a connection with your subject. Verbally ask them for permission to examine their aura and to share your perceptions.

STEP ONE: **Conduct Spirit-to-Spirit.** Affirm your personal spirit and then acknowledge the spirit of your subject, as well as the spiritual guidance that accompanies them. Finally, affirm the Spirit, surrendering this exercise to the Spirit and its approved spiritual assistants.

STEP TWO: **Concentrate on Your Third Eye.** For this exercise, I recommend that you close your eyes. This will eliminate distractions. Then breathe deeply and concentrate on your third eye. Relax and ask that the Spirit clear your mind.

STEP THREE: **Request and Interpret an Image.** Ask the Spirit to grant you an image of your subject's auric field. Analyze the vision for the applicable features discussed in the last chapter and earlier in this one. Factors include figuring out if you are perceiving the entire aura (full sight) or part of it (half sight). You might also want to double-check for sources of the vision and point of view, although, most likely, you'll initially be operating in third-person limited. Evaluate for color, shape, and form. Check to see if there are holes, weak areas, leaks, or attachments. Look also to see if there are symbols in the field or if the field is linked to someone else's field. If you require additional pictures or insights, ask for these as well.

STEP FOUR: **Share Interpretations.** Share your perspectives with the subject. If you feel hesitant about one of your ideas, pause and ask the Spirit to provide you an additional image. It's okay to request feedback from the subject, asking questions like "Does what I'm saying mean anything to you?" You can also ask the subject to throw their own questions in the mix. See if new visions appear when they do this. Continue with your interaction until you feel done.

STEP FIVE: **Close.** Thank your subject aloud for this interaction and silently affirm the Spirit for the aid. Release yourself and your subject from this session.

Classical Clairvoyance
EXTERNAL VISIONS

I'm old enough to remember the classical phrase uttered in cartoons when Superman was spotted in the sky:

"Look! It's a bird. It's a plane. It's—*Superman*!"

Life is full of equivalent signs and wonders that can be spied with our physical eyes. Occurrences are considered clairvoyant if they are visual and hold a deeper supernatural rather than only natural meaning. The bearers of these clairvoyant messages include beings from the natural world such as animals, plants, birds, and reptiles; elements, which might appear as a rush of wind or just-stilled water; events in our habitat or environment such as an object falling in front of us; and visuals that become obvious in our surroundings. The latter category includes messages perceived on a billboard, license plate, or flyer, as well as words in a manuscript or on the internet. We might also spy ghostly emanations in the environment. If any of these or similar visual manifestations occur in a way that seems imperative, meaningful, sudden, or repetitive, we might want to take notice and figure out the message.

Before interpreting an environmental image, we have to figure out if it's the genuine article. I might see a tree full of crows and that's all it is, a tree full of crows. Then again, that particular flock of birds might be conveying an important message—as one flock did recently.

I was walking my dogs in a park and dozens of crows congregated on an oak tree. Eerily, they began cawing. I felt chilled and scared. I'd just been wondering if a new acquaintance was a safe individual to spend time with. If you do an internet search for the phrase "the spiritual meaning of crows," you'll read that crows represent mystery and magic, but also cunning and death. The symbology of the crow, along with my unease, prompted me to cut off contact with this individual. I later learned that he had a habit of stalking women.

There is no limit to the types of beings that can deliver visual messages through our surroundings. In addition to living beings and environmental cues, we'll obviously pay attention if a ghost or an angel appears in our room. These types of figures don't always look like the images in picture books or photographs; sometimes they materialize as shadows, lights, or colorful shapes. To know who or what is appearing, you can use the types of exercises in this book, such as the one immediately following this section. A word of advice, however: don't limit your sense of who or what might visualize in front of you. In fact, God once visited me in the form of a flaming male. That's right—a man made of fire. I was traveling in England and this figure, who I could visibly see, kept shaking my bed. I was upset at being awoken and admit to swearing a bit. After the being told me that he was God, I felt chagrined. The visual disappeared, but I had the strong sense that the presence of the Divine remained with me like an invisible companion for the next several days.

An interesting visual that many people see are orbs, which are colorful balls of light that can pop into a room or appear on photographs. Usually an orb is a friendly spirit. It might be an angel, a guardian being, or a deceased loved one. For example, I was once teaching a class in Chicago and talking about fairies. Wind rushed into the enclosed room, and dozens of rainbow-colored balls swirled in. They flew around and then disappeared. I thought it interesting that only about half the class could perceive the orbs. Some of us are able to see visual beings and some are not. As well, our visualization ability is affected by our beliefs. If we don't believe in fairies—or totems or the like—it might be harder to attract or spy them.

Before you can interpret an environmental sign—including the sudden appearance of a being of nature, ghostly visitor, or even an interesting license plate—you need to make sure that it's delivering a genuine clairvoyant message. In general, I consider an occurrence an external vision if it meets any of these criteria:

- appears suddenly or unexpectedly
- shows up three or more times

- fills you with a sense of meaning or emotion

- reminds you of something or someone from the past

- makes you think about something or someone important to you right now

- makes you think about a desire you hold for the future

- seems out-of-sync with "normal reality"

- stimulates a supernatural or paranormal feeling

- initiates an evolved or mystical state

- remains in your mind long after the sighting

Once you've determined that you need to pay attention to what's showing up, it's helpful to distinguish between the two main types of messages it might be conveying. The two types are as follows:

OMEN: An event that might happen in the future, positive or negative. These are also called portents, especially if a negative event is being indicated.

SIGN: An indicator conveying information or instructions.

How might you know the difference between these two basic styles? Pretend that you are thinking about a friend's upcoming wedding and a storm blows in out of nowhere. You check in with the Spirit and see an image suggesting that there is a supernatural message provided for you. The question remains, does the storm qualify as an omen or a sign?

As you ask the question, you are provided an internal clairvoyant image of your friend's wedding date. You watch as the skies open up and her garden wedding is drenched. *Ah*, you think, *this is an omen.* Maybe you tell your friend to make sure that she orders a tent for that special day. Let's imagine that instead you receive a psychic vision of you and your husband fighting. In this case, the very-real storm in the environment represents a challenge in your very-real marriage and is a sign.

How do you know how to interpret environmental sightings? The internet is replete with helpful sites relating to natural harbingers. Simply look up the spiritual meaning of whatever you've spotted. The next two exercises will help you more thoroughly analyze an external message or more actively seek a sign or omen.

Analyzing a Sign

Have you spied a possible sign or omen through your physical or psychic eyes? In this exercise I'm going to use the term "sign" to represent both possibilities. Using all the qualifiers that you've learned so far, perform an assessment via the following steps.

PREPARE: You might be physically viewing a sign or remembering a sign that you've seen. Either way, take a few moments to relax.

STEP ONE: **Conduct Spirit-to-Spirit.** Acknowledge your personal essence, the helpers' spirits, and the Spirit. Affirm that you want insight regarding the applicability and meaning of the sign.

STEP TWO: **Ask Questions.** Request that the Spirit respond to the following questions with additional psychic visions:

- Is this a genuine sign? (What might a psychic no look like? Your eyes will wander away from the harbinger or the psychic

CHAPTER 3

image might disappear. A psychic yes will be
packaged as a psychic vision that's strong. If
the visitation doesn't qualify as a sign, quit
this exercise and thank the Spirit for the
clarity.)

- Is this sign meant for me? If not, should I
assess it? (Again, your physical or psychic
eyes will lose focus if you aren't supposed
to analyze the sign. If the sign is meant for
someone else, ask who. Then check to see
if you are supposed to proceed or not.)

- What is the source of this sign?

- What type of sign is it? (omen or sign)

- What does the sign mean?

- Can I get additional images to explain the
sign?

- What might occur if I ignore this sign?

- How am I to further understand this sign?

- Are there additional questions I should ask
from the list beginning on page 77?

- If the sign is related to someone else, am
I supposed to share my perceptions with
them?

STEP THREE: **Respond.** Decide how you want to respond practically to your newly acquired insights. If pertinent, ask for healing streams of grace.

STEP FOUR: **Close.** Thank the Spirit, all other spirits, and your own spirit for assistance. If you are confused about the meaning of a sign, trust your instincts. They won't lead you wrong.

Exercise
-9-

Seeking a Sign
THE EVERYDAY VISION QUEST

What if you want to seek out a physical sign? I do so all the time by conducting an everyday vision quest.

The term "vision quest" was assigned by anthropologists to describe a traditional rite-of-passage ceremony used amongst many indigenous cultures to ask the Spirit for insight. One particular type of Native American vision quest has been conducted the same way for hundreds of years amongst some tribes.

When a boy reaches puberty, elders leave him in the wild for three days. During this time the boy prays, asking for a totem to reveal a message from the Spirit. Nature responds, perhaps with a visitation of an animal, bird, or reptile, or maybe by striking the ground with a bolt of lightning. Whatever appears provides a clue about the boy's essential purpose and powers.

You can conduct a vision quest for yourself, but you don't have to climb a mountaintop to do so. This vision quest can be inserted into your everyday life. The only requirement is a willingness to allow the Spirit to grant you a sign through the environment. Simply take the following steps:

PREPARE: Decide what issue you'd like to focus upon, and then select a time period in which you'd like to receive a sign or omen. I usually conduct the quest for three days to a week.

STEP ONE: **Perform Spirit-to-Spirit.** Affirm your own spirit, the spirits of others—including the beings that will help deliver a message—and the Spirit. Ask the Spirit to bring you a sign during the selected time frame that will shed insight on your issue.

STEP TWO: **Remain Open.** Be aware of your environment. Notice the unusual appearance of a specific animal or other living being. Look for odd events, paying attention to visual cues such as meaningful license plates and billboards. Also remain open to psychic means of communication such as astounding nightly dreams or daydreams. You can use the advice and exercises in the next section, Classical Clairvoyance: Nighttime and Daytime Dreams, to analyze any dreams.

STEP THREE: **Assess.** Work with the strongest of the signs that appear. Write about it. Pray and meditate on it. Research totems or other matters on the internet. Gain the insight that has been sent to you by spending time in meditation using the Analyzing a Sign exercise provided earlier in this chapter.

STEP FOUR: **Close.** At the end of the time period, thank the Spirit and any beings that worked with the Spirit to help you.

Classical Clairvoyance
Nighttime and Daytime Dreams

On November 10, 1619, Renee Descartes, mathematician, scientist, and metaphysician, experienced a series of three dreams. He awoke from the first dream confused and disturbed. In it, he was being pursued by ghosts. He calmed down upon entering a college. The second dream featured a clap of thunder. The third dream showcased two different books, a dictionary and a tome of poetry. The dictionary was missing pages, however, and Descartes surmised that the poetry book contained the information he was truly seeking (Dennis 2010).

From these three dreams, Descartes derived his life purpose, which resulted in him becoming the father of empirical science. He decided to reform knowledge and pursue reason as his god. From my assessment of his dreams, I would suggest that the first dream initiated his quest, symbolizing a search for safety and knowledge. I interpret the second dream as an awakening. The third dream told Descartes where he'd find true wisdom—in poetry, the musings of the conscious.

Descartes' three dreams hint at what's available for us through clairvoyant dreams, whether we receive them during the night or as daydreams. I received clarity as to my own purpose during a dream I had when traveling in Morocco.

In that particular nighttime dream, I saw God wearing tennis shoes. He was scribbling on a chalkboard. He then turned around to look at me, as if to say, "You getting this?" Then he began drawing outside of the board's bounds. "This is your job," he ordered me. "To tell people what exists out here."

Besides serving as vehicles for information, our nighttime dreams are a perfect forum for interacting with guides. I still recall one dream in which a group of angels put me through an emotional event. Then they pulled me out of the dream (I was still asleep) and showed me that I had been in a movie set. Then they stuck someone else in the set! I got the message. Life provides us whatever props we need to deal with our inner emotions.

During our nighttime dreams, we might also conduct soul journeys and probe our psychological issues, amongst other activities. Even if you don't remember your dreams, you have them.

Daydreams can also consist of clairvoyant images. I had a client sell her house and move to Europe because of a daydream. She was doing paperwork in her law office and was struck by a psychic image. In it, a huge angel appeared and told her that she needed to shift into her "real work." The angel revealed an image of Paris and then disappeared.

My client had studied French literature in college and had always wanted to be a college professor. After the daydream, she applied for a master's program in Paris, sold her house to finance her studies, and moved to Paris to study.

Do you want to understand your dreams, either daydreams or night dreams? The next exercise, Analyzing a Clairvoyant Dream, can be used to comprehend a daydream or night dream. The exercise following it, Requesting a Clairvoyant Nighttime Dream, will help you request a clairvoyant dream when sleeping.

Exercise
--10--

Analyzing a Clairvoyant Dream

Do you long to figure out the meaning of a repetitive dream? Have you had an upsetting or an intriguing dream? Has a friend asked you to analyze their dream? Has a daydream captivated you? The easiest way to comprehend a dream, whether it be a daydream or nighttime dream, is to use the following process:

PREPARE: Grab a writing instrument and paper or use a computer. Write down everything you can remember about the dream.

STEP ONE: **Conduct Spirit-to-Spirit.** Affirm your personal spirit, those of the guides called to assist you, and the Spirit. Ask that all three types of essences work together to provide accurate insights. Know that you'll be granted visions in response to the following questions or areas of interest and that you can write down your reflections.

STEP TWO: **Source the Image.** Check with the Spirit. Does it approve of the source of the dream or not? What is the source of the dream? If a source is negative or undesirable, ask the Spirit to release you from that source and send healing streams to repair your psyche and boundaries. If the source is positive, you can continue. Otherwise, ask the Spirit to protect you from the harmful source.

STEP THREE: **Add More Elements.** Record all the important dream elements in list form. These qualifiers could include colors, characters, shapes, landscape, locations, events, interactions, your emotional reactions, and more.

STEP FOUR: **Analyze the Elements.** Review the list and ask the Spirit to relate meaning to each of the elements. Ask for a psychic vision to explain any of the elements you don't understand. Then ponder the overall meaning of these dream elements for a few moments and see if they add up to a central message.

STEP FIVE: **Analyze the Central Image.** If you are still unclear about the meaning of the dream, ask the Spirit to psychically show you an image depicting the core of the dream. Concentrate on this image and seek to understand its message. You can always request additional images. Write down your musings and conclusions.

STEP SIX: **Put It All Together.** Look over everything you've written and ask the Spirit to summarize the entire dream in a final picture. Spend time with this picture and pull counsel from it.

STEP SEVEN: **Request Healing Streams of Grace.**
Is there a reason for you or someone else to receive healing streams, based on the message in the vision? Now is the time to request these.

STEP EIGHT: **Close.** Thank the Spirit for the clarity and follow any advice culled from the dream.

Exercise
–11–

Requesting a Clairvoyant Nighttime Dream

You can deliberately foster a dream by setting the intention to do so. Gather paper and pencil and decide what you'd like to know about. Do you need answers to a question? An understanding about a relationship? Is there healing required or do you long for a visit by a spiritual guide? Write down your request and any additional thoughts about the issue.

Now mindfully prepare for bed. Take a bath, assure a quiet bedroom, and set the paper with your request near your bedside; also have a pen or pencil handy. At bedtime conduct Spirit-to-Spirit and ask the Spirit to grant you a dream during the night.

Upon awakening, if you've dreamed, record the images immediately and ask the Spirit to help you analyze the message in the dream. You can use the tips from the previous exercise, Analyzing a Clairvoyant Dream, to aid in interpretation. Even if you don't remember your dream, record whatever pops in your mind after awakening. Imagine that you had a dream, and a storyline will unfold.

You can conduct this activity several nights in a row, as classical clairvoyance often works best in dreamtime over a longer time period.

———

Now that you've learned the ins and outs of the colorful and fantastical classical clairvoyance, you are ready to learn about a different form of clairvoyance: prophecy. Get ready to evaluate visions for their deeper spiritual meanings.

Additional Questions

ADDING TO YOUR QUEUE

Chapter 2 concluded with a set of questions you can ask to understand a clairvoyant vision. You can add the following to that list, based on what you learned in this chapter:

- Can I receive more information to clarify the following? (You can add these factors to those listed under the same question on page 78.)

  ⋆ colors (clear or "off" colorations)

  ⋆ attachments such as cords or curses

  ⋆ symbols (shapes or numbers)

  ⋆ locations (landscapes, chakric/field, bodily, or any others that stand out)

  ⋆ supportive tools to use (foods, stones/objects, or oils)

• • • • • • •

Summary

Classical clairvoyance is managed by the sixth chakra, which relays visions that are colorful. In this chapter you prepared to work with the three main types of classical clairvoyance—inner visions, external visions, and dreams—by analyzing the meaning of colors, symbols, and locations.

You were also introduced to a few focusing tools, including foods, stones and other objects, and essential oils. Then you learned a variety of techniques to access each of the three main classical clairvoyant styles.

Adding this chapter's newly found information to the techniques garnered from chapter 2 marks you as a truly classical clairvoyant.

CHAPTER FOUR

The Path of Prophetic Visioning

How does clairvoyant prophecy differ from classical clairvoyance? That's the subject we'll be addressing in this chapter. Just wait until you understand the sheer magnificence of your prophetic ability! You'll be more than delighted that you spent time to comprehend and develop it.

By the time you are done with this chapter, you'll have a strong sense of the beauty and power of prophetic clairvoyance, or prophetic visioning. Ultimately, prophetic visions are spiritual in nature. Images reflected through the corresponding seventh chakra are black, white, or gray. These hues inspire and reveal what the Spirit has to share.

Because the basic prophetic gift is empathic, few individuals even know that they can receive images through their seventh chakra. Individuals who do receive prophetic visions don't always recognize them for what they are and might even discount them, as they aren't vivid and colorful like classically clairvoyant images.

This chapter contains the information and coaching required to attune and apply your prophetic energy. After explaining what clairvoyant prophecy is, I then differentiate it from classical clairvoyance. I'll next share a simple exercise that will help you accelerate this amazing gift. My own experience with clairvoyant prophecy has left me with great respect for the aptitude. Essentially, clairvoyant prophecy reveals a path of light that will never lead us wrong.

Bearers of the Light
PICTURES OF PROPHECY

When most of us think about prophets, we picture the gray-bearded, robed seers from the Abrahamic religions or envision gurus sharing wisdom along the banks of the Ganges River. The truth is that these examples are few and far between, at least in the real world. But, in fact, life is full of everyday prophets, and if you are reading this book, you are most likely gifted in prophecy.

Prophets are "truth knowers." They are spiritually aware individuals who deliver messages on behalf of the Spirit. Their ultimate job is to activate another's divine nature and help them align with the Spirit. Prophets consider all life areas as fair game, offering advice about career, love, sexual identity, spiritual guidance, vocational calling, and other matters.

Prophecy is most often experienced as spiritual knowledge or higher empathy. When being prophetic, an individual usually becomes consciously aware of what is best for themselves or others. They receive their messages, which are ultimately body-based, from their own spirit, others' spiritual guides, or the Spirit. You'll notice that these three elements are the same as those involved in Spirit-to-Spirit. As you might guess, the Spirit-to-Spirit technique is exceptionally suitable for gaining prophetic knowledge.

You've probably accessed your prophetic empathy hundreds, if not thousands, of times, even if you haven't had a label for the sensitivity. Have you ever sensed that a friend was on the verge of greatness or joy, especially if they took a certain job, went on a particular upcoming date, or aimed at a goal? Or maybe you felt that someone wasn't what they appeared to be. In the end, truth was revealed and your inner awareness was proven accurate.

I have a perfect example of sensory-based prophecy. Years ago, a friend called me. He wasn't feeling well.

I sensed that he should be tested for Lyme disease. He did. The result was negative. Something didn't feel right about the test results, so I suggested that he get reexamined. This time the blood panel revealed Lyme disease. He could now get treated.

For me, the challenge of relying on the standard empathic version of prophecy is that it's difficult to trust an awareness. Prophecy essentially involves downloading what the Spirit knows, as if transferring data from an iPhone onto a laptop. The knowledge of God surpasses what we can comprehend or corroborate with our brain. It's hard to logically validate prophetic insights, and it usually takes a while before they are proven right. Because of factors like these, many of us squelch our prophetic inclinations; neither do we want to appear foolish, mislead someone, or eventually be shown as wrong.

Nonetheless, prophecy is a reliable means for connecting to the Spirit's guidance and enabling values-based decisions. Because of this, prophecy is usually prescriptive, in that the revelations suggest what might occur if we do X rather than Y. These are a few of the reasons that we want to tap into—and rely upon—our prophetic abilities.

A little-known fact about the prophetic gift is that it can be psychically accessed visually, not only empathically. In fact, the seventh chakra, the home of prophecy, is biologically designed to enable visualization, or clairvoyance. The images will appear differently than those formed within the sixth chakra. Seventh versus sixth chakra images will also accomplish different purposes. If you've been mainly delving into your prophetic sense through awareness, consider supplementing with prophetic vision. And if you don't know if you've ever seen—or know how to see—through the seventh chakra, you're in a good place. You'll love this process and benefit considerably.

How the Seventh Chakra Sees the Sights

How exactly does the seventh chakra package insights as clairvoyant pictures? The answer lies in an explanation of the pineal gland, the hormone gland associated with the seventh chakra.

Shaped like a pine cone, hence the name "pine-al," the pineal is a small endocrine gland located in between the two brain hemispheres. Its placement suggests that biologically and metaphysically the pineal assists with balancing our feminine/intuitive and masculine/logical traits. Besides assuring internal connectivity, this gland manages several vital life areas. It produces hormones that regulate mood, sleep, sexual development, and several aspects of reproduction. It also secretes a cascade of hormones that are linked to the higher states of consciousness leading toward enlightenment. Enlightenment occurs when we realize that we are—and have always been—unified with and loved by the Spirit and others' spirits. This awareness invites us to express our divine nature in all that we do.

The pineal gland is also sensitive to light. Little wonder that many mystics and sages throughout the ages have considered it the center of clairvoyant vision and why Descartes, the scientist we met in the last chapter, called it the seat of the soul. I believe that colorful visions emanate from the sixth chakra but that you can also create or receive clairvoyant images via the seventh chakra, not only because of the spiritualizing hormones produced by the pineal, but also because of its basic biological link to light.

From an organic viewpoint, the pineal gland is an atrophied photoreceptor. This means that it is a vestigial organ for sight. Vestigial organs are those that were well-developed in earlier eras but no longer serve all of their innate functions. The implication is that once upon a time, humans relied on the pineal gland for vision.

Humans aren't the only species with a pineal gland. Animals also have pineal glands, but it's the presence of the pineal gland in amphibians and reptiles that shines the clearest light on the subject.

Present in dinosaurs, the pineal gland is even now found in lizards, frogs, sharks, and various other species, where it functions as a parietal eye—or a third eye. Mechanically, a parietal eye has a lens, cornea, retina, and a primitive optic nerve that links the eye to the brain. This eye performs many important functions. It can detect threats from shadows, perceive polarized light (which are waves of light on a single plane), navigate the environment, and regulate circadian rhythms (Quantumbiologist 2010). The biological imprint of the parietal eye hints at why humans can access clairvoyant energy through the seventh chakra.

Seventh chakra visions aren't colorful, although the seventh chakra is capable of passing polarized or simple light into the sixth chakra's structures, which can then convert them into multidimensional images. However, the stand-alone pictures generated by the seventh chakra consist of a continuum of white light, ranging from the brightest of whites on one end to the darkest of blacks on the other—exactly how images are perceived through many species' parietal eyes. Through my work I've determined that the white energies reflect the most optimum spiritual choices and the black energies represent the least effective spiritual options. The various shades of gray indicate a mixture of hidden knowledge.

What might purely prophetic visions look and operate like? I'll give you two examples.

I was recently pondering if I should attend a baseball tournament or not. My son's club baseball team had qualified, but the costs would be astronomical. My options were to send him alone or to accompany him.

I conducted Spirit-to-Spirit and focused on my seventh chakra. I didn't want a complicated sixth chakra image; I only wanted Spirit's reaction to my question. Was it spiritually beneficial for all concerned to have me attend the four-day event or not?

Immediately I was shown the imprint of a ball field on my mind screen. It was light white, indicating that the tournament was a positive event. I perceived a silhouette of my son on the field. He was shiny white, which affirmed that he should go. Then I saw a figure I knew to be me. I was also bright white. I had my answer. I purchased an airplane ticket and flew to Florida with my son.

The trick with clairvoyant prophecy is that you don't really know what the Spirit has in mind with a thumb's up. I only figured out the reason during the event.

Right from the beginning, I became the team's den mother. I collected baseball kids who were traveling alone at the two airports we flew into and arrived in Florida with four young men in tow. The car rental manager looked at me and the four hulking boys with all their gear and gave me a free upgrade. Because I now had an eight-person van, I was appointed chauffeur. Day and night I drove kids to games, restaurants, and the beach. If I hadn't attended, no one else would have been on hand to drive them around.

I use clairvoyant prophecy to make personal decisions as well as to hone in on prescriptive insights for clients. As discussed in chapter 2, prescriptive rather than descriptive visions are those that reveal the highest outcome. A client requested input about whether to vacation in California or Washington State. I was first shown several sixth chakra visions that showcased tourist sites from both states. These images weren't going to help my client make a solid decision. Clearly, both states offered a lot of fun activities. So I asked for an assessment through my seventh chakra.

Immediately I saw a side-by-side image of the two states. There was a gray film over California and a white light over Washington State. I shared the vision with my client, explaining the meaning of the hues, and she decided to visit Washington State—which was a good thing. The area of California that she would have visited was struck with fires during her vacation time.

One of the keys to accessing the clairvoyant powers of your seventh chakra is keeping in mind the difference between sixth and seventh chakra visions. I'll talk a little bit more about this next.

Sixth Versus Seventh Chakra Visions
WHAT'S THE DIFFERENCE?

In general, sixth chakra visions depict situations across the past, present, and the future, and they always feature at least one rainbow color. They can be descriptive (providing data) or prescriptive (providing insights to destiny). Overall, seventh chakra pictures are prescriptive, providing insight or inspiration for decision-making. They can address circumstances related to the past, present, or the future, but the advice given usually pertains to the decision at hand. As well, the seventh chakra aspect of the vision will appear on a continuum of white to black.

Many times, the sixth and seventh chakras interrelate to formulate a mixed vision or set of pictures. For example, a friend of mine was trying to decide if she should sell her house or not. I guided her through Spirit-to-Spirit so that she could connect with her own intuitive guidance.

First, she psychically pictured her current house. She noticed a black cloud in the roof. Then she was shown a map of a certain suburb. There was a beautiful fog of white over that suburb. Based on the black versus white imagery, she sold her house and bought a new one in the indicated area. A couple of months after she moved, a storm struck her old neighborhood. A great big oak tree was hit by lightning and fell on the roof. She had been spared the cleanup and perhaps also something worse. Although the current residents of her former house weren't injured, my client had often slept in an attic room. Had she remained in the house, she might have been hurt or even killed.

The following table highlights the basic comparisons between sixth and seventh chakra visions:

FUNCTION	SIXTH CHAKRA	SEVENTH CHAKRA
Overall purpose:	Descriptive or prescriptive	Usually prescriptive
Time periods:	Past, present, and future; explanatory in nature	Past, present, and future; gives values-based advice
Images:	Always colorful and can also feature shapes, symbols, forms, and more	Only black, white, and gray
Sources:	Multi-level and cross-dimensional	Ideally, only the Spirit and the Spirit's emissaries
Used for:	Information gathering	Guidance for decision-making

Now that you better understand prophetic clairvoyance, your source of spiritual advice and insight, it's time to figure out how to tap in to this amazing resource for yourself. The following exercise is designed to help you do just that.

Getting a Prophetic Vision

The key to accessing prophetic visions is to fully attune the pineal gland and the overall seventh chakra to the Spirit. In this exercise I'll relay a simple way to acclimate your seventh chakra and receive a response from the Spirit to a query. You can use this exercise to open to a voluntarily requested vision or to respond to an involuntarily obtained vision. I'll simply show you where to insert the already-received psychic picture.

This exercise will help you take advantage of a unique relationship between your pineal gland and the cosmos. Many cultures and scientists believe that the pineal gland interacts with the greater universe. We know that it responds to environmental light and also reacts to universal vibrations through a process called rhythm entrainment, or resonance. According to the Taoists, followers of an ancient Chinese philosopher, the North Star is the source of the world's original pulsations. Even now, the vibrations of the North Star, amongst other stellar bodies, are said to emanate vibrations that support life on earth (Chia and Thom 2016). To take advantage of the pineal gland's celestial connections, this exercise will assist you in establishing the highest resonance possible.

PREPARE: Find a quiet space in which to reflect through your seventh chakra. Make sure you won't be disturbed, then settle into your body and take a few deep breaths.

STEP ONE: **Conduct Spirit-to-Spirit.** Affirm your spirit, the spirit of others' involved with your process, and the Spirit.

STEP TWO: **Focus on Your Seventh Chakra.** Bring your attention to your seventh chakra, located at the top of your head. In particular, ask the Spirit to relate to you through your pineal gland.

STEP THREE: **Align Your Seventh Chakra.** Ask the Spirit to clear and cleanse your seventh chakra, including the pineal gland. Request that the Spirit fill your seventh chakra with spiritual light, specifically attuning it with the streams of grace needed to help this chakra resonate with the most beautiful energies of the world, including the higher heavens. Enjoy this interconnectivity as long as you desire.

STEP FOUR: **Frame a Question.** What topic is on
your mind? Is there a decision you'd like to
make? A deceased relative to check in on? Maybe there is a problem you need to reflect upon.
Frame your request. Pose your question to
allow a black-and-white, values-based response.
For instance, if you need help with a decision
about buying a car or not, you can ask, "Does
this car support my higher destiny?" If you want
to figure out how your deceased grandfather is
doing on the other side, you can ask, "What is
the state of my grandfather's soul right now?"

   If you've received a prophetic vision previously, you can insert that particular image into
the process in this step and design a question
aimed at interpreting that vision.

STEP FIVE: **Receive the Vision.** Remain composed
while the Spirit shares a vision that responds to
your request. It will appear in shades of white to
black. If part of the vision comes from the sixth
chakra, ask the Spirit to separate out the sixth
chakra insights so you can focus only on those
produced by the seventh chakra.

STEP SIX: **Assess the Vision.** Reflect upon the vision. Where are the obvious white areas? Are there any black or gray areas?

You can assess the vision using many of the tips covered in chapter 2. Make sure that the vision is true rather than fantastical. If it's fantastical, ask for a true vision. Figure out if the image is literal or metaphorical and also double-check the source by requesting an additional image. If it's not Spirit-approved, you'll perceive a black energy. Ask the Spirit to clear the shadow and become the sole information source.

Also evaluate for the type of sight you are using—first, second, third limited, or third omniscient, as well as half or full sight. Alter viewpoints if it seems that trying a new scene would be helpful. Ask about time periods.

Then evaluate the black, white, or gray areas. As for additional clarifying visions for black or white areas. Ask to perceive the information underlying a gray area. At this point, you can also ask for a classical clairvoyant image to further understand any mysteries.

STEP SEVEN: **Close.** When you've received the desired input, thank the Spirit and helping spirits for the assistance. Ask the Spirit to integrate any energies sent your way, then ask that your seventh chakra continue to resonate beautifully and safely with the greater cosmos. Take a few deep breaths and go about your day.

Additional Tip
QUARTZ IT UP

Do you want to bolster a prophetic picture? White quartz crystals, as well as Herkimer and traditional diamonds, add sparkle to a prophetic vision. While conducting Spirit-to-Spirit, hold a clear stone in your hand. Ask the Spirit to send streams of grace through the stone and into your hand and body. These streams will flow into your pineal gland, brightening your interactions.

After you've finished the exercise, wash the stone in water and ask the Spirit to cleanse it with healing streams. You can use the stone again at a different time.

———

Now that you've had a wondrous experience with your seventh chakra, you are ready to master other empathic gifts from a clairvoyant perspective.

Additional Questions

ADDING TO YOUR QUEUE

Do you want a few more questions for your developing Q&A? Add these, which pertain to prophetic images, to those presented at the end of chapters 2 and 3:

- Would it be helpful to transform a classical clairvoyant image into a prophetic image or vice versa?

- If this image is prophetic, I request to be shown another image to explain these hues:

  * black
  * white
  * gray

• • • • • • •

Summary

The seventh chakra is the home of spiritual empathy, through which we become aware of the Spirit's knowledge and insight. This chakra's special relationship with the pineal gland, an atrophied photoreceptor, enables prophetic visioning. These seventh chakra images differ from the sixth chakra's visions in that they appear in shades of black, white, and gray rather than colors, and they enable us to follow the Spirit's marching orders. Black indicates unsuitable choices, white shows optimum ideas, and gray suggests hidden knowledge.

We can turn to our seventh chakra when we want inspiration and insight directly from the Spirit or the Spirit's highest helpers.

• • • •

CHAPTER FIVE

Empathic Visioning
FROM EMPATHY
TO VISION

Much of our mystical knowledge is received empathically. Empathy is commonly defined as the ability to relate to someone or something else, but it's actually a bit more complicated than that. Certainly, empathy involves sensing what's occurring with others, but it also includes relating to parts of ourselves—body, mind, and soul—through our own bodily sensations.

We discussed one particular type of empathy in the last chapter: spiritual empathy. Through spiritual empathy, we receive values-based revelation. There are four additional types of empathy, each of which is housed in one of the seven in-body chakras. In this chapter we will specifically address these empathic styles, which are physical, feeling, mental, and relational.

Kinesthetic awareness makes us human and can call forth the best of our humanity, including compassion and care. But when we're trying to figure out the source and meaning of empathic impression, it's easy to feel lost—which is why it's so great to turn empathic sensations into pictures.

Is that pain in your toe caused by too-tight shoes? Or is your toe "sharing" a message, say, that you need to step forward and take more chances?

How about a churning gut? Are your intestines sour because you've done something distasteful or because they've absorbed someone else's emotions?

Most people are highly empathic but struggle with defining the meaning of a sensation, whether it is primarily physical, emotional, mental, or relational. That's where clairvoyance comes in. By transforming an empathic knowing into a psychic vision, you can better understand and analyze the sensation. You can figure out if a feeling belongs to you or someone else. You can decide if it's important to pay attention to a "knowing" or to let it go. You can mine for more data. Stated plainly, you can manage your empathic sensitivities rather than be governed by them.

In this chapter I'll first explore two basic sources of empathic sensations, which are external or internal. I'll then describe the four main types of empathic knowledge, providing examples of each and exploring their chakric and auric field relationships. Finally, I'll share a number of exercises that will introduce clairvoyance into your empathic endeavors. The first exercise will help you separate your own sensations from those of others. The second can be used to transform internal empathic knowledge into a psychic vision, so you can work with it. I'll also show you how to use drawing to explore empathic knowledge. To be empathic is a good thing, but how much better it is to actually understand what we're sensing!

Empathic Knowledge
THE TWO MAIN SOURCES

"My main problem is that I can't tell if I'm feeling my own feelings or someone else's," the young woman complained.

I know what that's like; so do many people. Not only can it be challenging to differentiate between our own and others' feelings, but we can also absorb others' physical pains, illnesses, motivations, mental chatter, belief systems, relational knowledge, and healing needs. For example, I once worked with a man who was experiencing aches and pains at night but never during the day. The throbbing sensations moved around his body, creating tender areas that hurt all night long. Sometimes he would cry as well, but he never knew what he was processing. He'd had an easy childhood and was therefore emotionally balanced. As well, he had no obvious illness. So what could be the cause of the strange sensations?

I conducted Spirit-to-Spirit and asked for an image to explain the man's pain. I envisioned a woman sleeping next to him. I assumed that this woman was his wife. He did too.

I asked if his wife experienced physical pain at night, and the client said that she didn't. I knew that this wasn't a fait accompli, however. Empathically, sensations can pass from one person or being to another. In these cases, the originator is often freed from their sensations. So I requested another picture from the Spirit. This time I saw a car accident.

The client stated that his wife had been in an accident during their first year of marriage. Though the event was violent, his wife had never seemed too physically or emotionally impacted by it. Upon prompting, the husband admitted that his pain and anguish had started after her accident. Most likely, my client had absorbed his wife's pain as a subconscious way to care for her.

We absorb others' energies in the same way that we take in any psychic or subtle energy, as explained in chapter 1. We can't process energies that aren't our own. Once stuck, the internalized energy can cause disease, psychological trauma, confusion, healing challenges, and spiritual maladies, among other problems.

I explained how energetic absorption works to my client. It made sense to him. We then used a version of the Visually Releasing the Empathic Energies of Others exercise (presented later in this chapter) to help him picture the pain and release it. Subsequently, his nighttime aching stopped. Gradually, his wife started to physically and emotionally process the accident. Because the exercise employs healing streams of grace to return energy to its owner, the pain was easily and safely reintegrated in the wife. The truth is that we do someone a favor by sending their energy back to them. We all have something to learn from everything.

The example just provided demonstrates what occurs when an empathic sensation is made up of another's internalized energy. Empathic impressions can also originate inside ourselves. In this case, they involve the communication from a physical, emotional, mental, or relational aspect of ourselves to the rest of us.

For instance, I had a client come to see me because she awoke every morning with a sore shoulder. She'd been to one doctor after another, including a chiropractor, all of whom tried different remedies. Nothing made a difference.

When this client came to see me, I had her take a few minutes and concentrate on the shoulder. She imagined that it was morning, and immediately her shoulder started to ache. I then used a version of the exercise found in this chapter, Transforming an Empathic Sensation into a Psychic Vision, to help her convert the soreness into a psychic image.

She envisioned her grandfather, who had died when she was ten. She'd been particularly close to her grandfather, who had been a mystic. He had used symbols to perform healing work. One morning before he died her grandfather had whispered, "I'm going to leave you my legacy" and clutched her shoulder.

After sharing this information, my client blanched. "Do you think I've been feeling—his legacy?"

I suggested that my client was feeling her grandfather's "charge" every morning. Maybe the pain would clear up if she started intuitively bringing through her grandfather's knowledge? I had my client awaken every morning and ask for pictures relaying her grandfather's mystical legacy. I also asked her to sketch the images and write about them. She followed my advice.

When she returned in a month, she had filled out several notepads with drawings of symbols as well as information. Her shoulder had completely stopped hurting. Having delivered the message, her shoulder didn't need to "speak" anymore. My client decided to write a book of her grandfather's esoteric knowledge.

So far, I've made two important points. The first is that the body can psychically take on energy from others and experience the information as empathic sensations. The sources of this energy can be other individuals but also any living being, including animals, plants, celestial forms, otherworldly beings, and objects. The second vital point is that empathic sensations can be communiqués from ourselves to ourselves. A gurgling stomach might mean nothing more than that we're hungry—then again, it might be explaining something important to us.

In order to apply clairvoyance in the empathic arena, it's beneficial to differentiate between the four main ways of being kinesthetic. Let's take a look at these four empathy styles.

The Four Forms of Empathy
HOW WE KNOW WHAT WE KNOW

What do all those bodily sensations mean? We all get them—a medley of physical, feeling, mental, and relational perceptions. These empathic sensations occur constantly and show that we are receiving communications from outside and inside of ourselves. You only need to analyze them, however, when they are especially strong, recurrent, problematic, or wondrous.

Every one of the four main empathic styles is managed by a distinct chakra and its corresponding auric field, is vulnerable to absorbing energy from others, and serves as a vessel for empathic messages for and from the self. As I more thoroughly describe these four styles, pay attention to which you might experience the most frequently. You can refer back to the information about the chakras in chapter 1 for additional chakra and auric field–based information.

Physical Empathy
(First Chakra and Auric Field)

The first chakra and auric field manage safety and security issues and all aspects of your physical and material existence. The related intuitive faculties are equally physical in nature. Through physical empathy, you can sense messages from the external world and from your physical self. These experiences are packaged as physical sensations, aches and pains, illness, waves of heat and cold, and bodily areas of pleasure. You might also receive psychic impressions sensed as touch, smell, taste, and other sensory stimulation. As well, physical empathy includes relating to the environment and objects. You might know what is happening inside of animals, plants, the earth, and the stars, and also pick up on energy emanating from an object. You may sense the physical states experienced by an aspect of yourself or another person or being, such as an inner child.

Feeling Empathy
(Second Chakra and Auric Field)

The chakra and auric field governing feeling empathy monitors our own and others' feelings, as well as creative efforts and expressions. When engaged in this type of empathy, you can pick up others' feelings and also relate to your own. Sources of feelings aren't restricted to other people or the self; they can also include sub-aspects of the self and others, otherworldly beings, and beings of nature.

Mental Empathy
(Third Chakra and Auric Field)

Want a thought or mental awareness, anyone? Mental empathy is resourced in the subtle structures devoted to beliefs, thoughts, mentality, and personal power. Because of this, mental empaths can relate to others' thoughts, motivations, deep-seated fears, prejudice, and goals. "Others" include people and their sub-aspects but also beings of nature and otherworldly characters. Empathic messages can also reference your own thoughts or motivations and truest desires and beliefs. These self-based messages can often be used to create a structure for success and increase self-esteem and self-confidence.

Relational Empathy
(Fourth Chakra and Auric Field)

There are two main empathic abilities demonstrated by relational empaths, the gift housed in the fourth chakra and field. In a nutshell, relational empaths can sense their own and others' relational and healing needs and love-based desires. Sources for this information include people but also esoteric and natural forces and beings. Relational empaths are often inspired to serve as healers or to make a difference in the lives of others.

———

Do you relate to any—or all—of these descriptions? Then you'll appreciate being able to perform two major activities. The first is to distinguish between your own and others' empathic sensations, and the other is to figure out how to interpret empathic messages. Exercises aimed at accomplishing these and similar goals finish out the rest of this chapter.

Exercise
—13—

Figuring Out the Ownership of an Empathic Sensation

How do you know if that sensation belongs to you or not? In some cases, empathic energy is made up of your own *and* another's energy, and you need to know this too.

This exercise will help you determine the nature of an empathic sense. If indicated, you can follow up by conducting one or both of the next exercises, Visually Releasing the Empathic Energies of Others and Transforming an Empathic Sensation into a Psychic Vision. To conduct this process, follow these very simple steps.

PREPARE: It's easiest to undergo this exercise in a private and quiet space. In a pinch, you can do it anywhere. To perform this exercise on the fly, in public, or during a conversation, ask for healing streams of grace to create subtle boundaries. In this way, you'll be secure while interacting in a tough or compelling situation.

STEP ONE: **Conduct Spirit-to-Spirit.** Acknowledge your own spirit, the spirits of those present (seen and unseen), and the Spirit. Ask that the Spirit take charge of this entire process.

STEP TWO: **Focus.** Concentrate on the physical, emotional, mental, or relational sensation you are experiencing. Breathe into the bodily area or the related chakra. You can use the tips in the next section to select a focal point.

STEP THREE: **Request an Image.** This is the most
important part of the exercise. Draw a box in
your mind and picture a vertical line going
down the middle. Now select a color to represent another's empathic energies and a different
color to exemplify your own empathic energies.

Ask the Spirit to perform two tasks. The first
is to fill in the left side of the box with the color
indicating another's energies. The second is to
fill in the right side of the box with the color
signifying your own energies. Left and right are
determined by your own viewpoint. The sides
of the box may or may not fill in completely—
or at all.

For amounts of any other proportion, work
with one or each of the two exercises already
recommended to gain empathic knowledge.
You can also use the exercise Drawing Empathically on page 181 to work with either side of
the box.

STEP FOUR: **Close.** Thank the Spirit and all helpers
for assisting you with this process.

Additional Tips

SELECTING A FOCUS FOR
AN EMPATHIC SENSATION

How do you know what to focus on when conducting an exercise involving empathic sensations? Following are a few tips that might help:

ISOLATE THE PAIN, PLEASURE, OR NUMB AREA:
You'll want to bring your consciousness to the bodily area that reverberates with a physical sensation. Sometimes, however, a bodily area is numb or lacking feeling and you'll want to focus on this site. You can always deliberate on the first chakra location in the coccyx, genitalia, or hip area if you can't pinpoint a particular physical site.

FEEL THE FEELING: If you are aware of an emotional distress in a bodily or chakra area, bring your attention there. Trust your body to guide you. If you're in doubt about the exact location of a feeling, attend to the second chakra.

KNOW WHAT YOU KNOW: We might think that we should focus on our head if we're flooded with mental chatter or unnerving ideas, but I encourage you to interact with your third chakra instead. Located in the solar plexus and mid back, this site disseminates our own and others' mental gossip, fears, and anxieties.

BE WHO YOU ARE: Issues related to relationships or healing always involve the heart. Center on the heart area if an empathic energy involves love at any level.

USE A FOCUS STONE: If you can't figure out what part of the body or system to relate to, hold a stone and picture the body's empathic energy pouring into it. I recommend using a clear or pink quartz stone, as both are pure energetic containers and won't taint what they receive. Now assume that the stone will reveal relevant and psychic clairvoyant messages to you. You can also ask that healing streams flow from the stone into you or anyone else.

Exercise
--14--

Visually Releasing the Empathic Energies of Others

The easiest way to release an empathic sensation that isn't your own is to first request a psychic picture, classical or prophetic, to explain why the energy is stuck in you. The second step is to employ healing streams. Via the streams, the Spirit will heal your issues, fill in holes left by the returned energy, and gently reintegrate another's energy back to them.

Sometimes you'll be able to decipher the origin of the empathic energy and sometimes not. This exercise will work either way.

PREPARE: Find a quiet place for this practice. If you need to perform it in public or quickly, ask for healing streams to support your energetic boundaries.

STEP ONE: **Conduct Spirit-to-Spirit.** Affirm your spirit, all other spirits, and the Spirit. If you've

already conducted the Figuring Out the Ownership of an Empathic Sensation exercise shared
earlier, picture the Spirit lifting the other's
energy out of the left side of the psychic box. If
you haven't conducted that exercise but know
that the empathic sensation isn't your own, ask
the Spirit to encapsulate the other's energy.

STEP TWO: **Ask for an Image.** Request that the
Spirit form the other's energy into a psychic
image that you can relate to. The picture might
be classical or prophetic. Now ask that Spirit
reveal insight or provide additional images,
responding to questions like these:

- What or who is the originator
  of this energy?
- Why have I been holding on to it?
- Is there a key to being willing
  to release the energy?

STEP THREE: **Let Go of the Other's Energy.** When
ready, give permission for the Spirit to return
the other's energy to them. Request that any
resulting holes inside your body, chakras, or
fields be restored with healing streams.

• • • •

If attachments are involved, you'll notice that the healing streams disintegrate the attachments, dissipating the cords, curses, or energy markers while sending grace to you and all involved parties. If you are using classical visioning, you might notice coloration changes. If your image is prophetic in nature, the vision will gradually turn light and white.

Remain in this process until you feel clear.

STEP FOUR: **Close.** Take a few moments and thank everything and everyone for aiding you. Then return to your normal life when ready.

Exercise
--15--

Transforming an Empathic Sensation into a Psychic Vision

What if an empathic sensation is a message from yourself to yourself? By transforming the sensation into a psychic vision, you can get the message and respond to it.

PREPARE: Find a quiet place and relax. Take a few deep breaths and focus on the empathic sensation calling attention to itself.

STEP ONE: **Conduct Spirit-to-Spirit.** Acknowledge your own spirit, the spirits of all involved, and the Spirit.

STEP TWO: **Focus on the Sensation.** With the Spirit's help, surrender to the sensation. Appreciate it. It contains a brilliant and vital message.

STEP THREE: **Create an Image.** Ask the Spirit to move the energy of the sensation into either your sixth or seventh chakra, thus changing the empathic energy into a classical or prophetic clairvoyant energy, respectively. As an image emerges, ask the Spirit to explain the empathic message. Use the techniques you've been taught in this book to better comprehend the meaning.

If it's a classical picture, analyze for color, shape, location, time periods, source, points of view, and more. If you are observing a prophetic vision, examine the shades of black, white, and gray, and any other factor that seems important. Ask for additional explanatory images, change points of view, and even shift from classical to prophetic visuals or vice versa.

Step Four: **Transform the Sensation.** Ask the Spirit how to best respond to the message shared from the empathic sensation. Visions will appear to direct you. Once you're clear about your personal responsibility, ask the Spirit to send streams of grace into the bodily and chakric regions that have been holding the empathic energy. Request that any unpleasant sensations be converted into neutral or positive energy. Know that these streams will remain connected as long as they are needed.

Step Five: **Close.** With appreciation for the assistance, breathe deeply and return to your everyday life.

Additional Tips

Receiving an Empathic Message from Spirits

Sometimes an empathic impression contains a message sent by spiritual guidance, otherworldly beings, or the Spirit. For instance, I once tuned in to a client and smelled roses. I shared this with him, and he began to cry. An image of his recently deceased sister popped in his mind; her favorite flower had been roses. She used the scent to reach through the veils to communicate with him.

What if the source of an empathic impression is spiritual? After performing Spirit-to-Spirit, you can analyze this matter with the following questions:

- Is the source of this empathic sensation Spirit-approved or not? (If not, ask for healing streams to release you from this source. You can also request an image to help explain how you became connected in the first place, what you can learn from the connection, and how to remain safe.)

- What is the message that this source is giving me?

- Why is this message showing up in an empathic form?

- How should I respond to this spiritual message?

- Can I have healing streams to transform these sensations after I have decided to pursue the spiritual advice or not?

Ask that your guidance provide any additional images needed and end this process when you feel done.

Additional Tip

OFFERING INSIGHT TO THE OWNER
OF THE EMPATHIC SENSATION

What if you are interacting with another person and are picking up on messages meant for—or emanating from—them? This occurs all the time to me, as I allow my body to relate to what's occurring within a client.

Quite simply, I employ the same processes already shared in this chapter. I conduct Spirit-to-Spirit, request a bolstering of my energetic boundaries, and then ask the Spirit to transform the other's energy into a psychic image that I can work with. I interact with the resulting image, whether it's classical or prophetic. I ask questions inside of my head, figure out sourcing, alter viewpoints, and share the perceptions I receive with the other person. I also ask the other person if the images mean anything to them.

Once we've jointly arrived at an interpretation, I ask for healing streams from the Spirit. These clear the empathically received energies I've picked up, and they also provide solace and assistant to the client. Then I thank all the spirits involved for this amazing interaction.

Drawing Empathically
RELEASING OR TRANSFORMING EMPATHIC SENSATIONS

This exercise teaches you how to draw your way into empathic understandings and changes.

PREPARE: To conduct this exercise, gather paper and crayons, colored pencils, or even just a pencil.

STEP ONE: **Find a quiet place and perform Spirit-to-Spirit.** Then focus on the bodily area in which you are sensing a physical, emotional, mental, or relational empathetic energy.

STEP TWO: **Draw a line down the middle of the paper.** Concentrate on the left side of the paper. It represents the energy of others. Follow your intuition and illustrate images, pictures, and the like that symbolize others' energies. You might or might not have anything to sketch. After all, the empathic sensation might only contain your own energy.

If the left side of your paper fills up, take another piece of paper and keep sketching. Label the papers so you can keep track of them.

STEP THREE: **Ask the Spirit to help you portray representations of personally empathic energies on the right side of the paper.** Get it all out! If needed, use additional papers, labeling them. See what appears when you ask for clarification of the empathic message. You can skip this step if all the energy belongs to someone or something else.

STEP FOUR: **Grab a new sheet of paper.** If another's energy was involved in the empathic sensation, use the entire piece of paper to reflect the Spirit's sharing of healing streams of grace. Then take a few moments and send personal blessings from your own spirit to the energy's owner, even as they are released from you.

If the empathic energies are your own, compose an image revealing what you'll feel, look, or be like once this energy has been completely transformed. Now sketch into the image the healing streams required to create the desired state. Add any other pictures needed, using additional sheets of paper, to enable transformation. When you are done, sense how different you feel.

———

Now that you've gained an understanding of the effect of empathy on your clairvoyance, it's time to add another amazing trick of the trade that connects your verbal capabilities to your visual aptitude.

Additional Questions
ADDING TO YOUR QUEUE

What types of questions will assist you in using visioning to better understand empathic sensations? The following questions can be added to those at the end of chapters 2, 3, and 4:

- Are the empathic sensations I'm feeling someone else's?

- Are the empathic sensations I'm feeling messages from spiritual sources?

- Are the empathic sensations I'm experiencing from myself to myself?

- Are there emotions, feelings, or understandings that can be turned into pictures to help me out?

  - ★ Are they physical in nature?

  - ★ Are they feelings-based in nature?

  - ★ Are they mental in nature?

  - ★ Are they relational in nature?

  - ★ Are they a mix of the four empathic styles?

• • • • • • •

Summary

Empathy is the means of relating to the outside world, although empathic sensations felt in the body can also provide messages from ourselves to ourselves, as well as from spiritual guides and the Spirit.

There are four main types of empathic sensations, each of which relates to a different chakra and related auric field. These are physical sensations (connected to the first chakra and auric field), emotional sensations (associated with the second chakra and auric field), mental sensations (anchored in the third chakra and auric field), and relational sensations (lodged in the fourth chakra and auric field).

In this chapter you learned that an empathic sensation can either contain energy that doesn't belong to you or energy that makes up a message (from yourself or spirits) that you need. You were shown several psychic visioning exercises useful for determining the nature of the empathic sensation and for returning or transforming it.

• • • •

CHAPTER SIX

Verbal Visioning
WHERE WORDS
MEET PICTURES

I love the phrase "A picture is worth a thousand words." Clairvoyants constantly prove the truth of this statement. However, sometimes adding a word or two to a picture makes the image mean much more.

Clairaudience (meaning "clear hearing") is a mystical gift equivalent to—but different from—clairvoyance. It involves audibly receiving guidance packaged as tones, words, songs, or other verbal means, as well as reading messages. Like clairvoyance, clairaudience works with psychic but also sensory energy.

A little-known fact in metaphysical communities is that clairvoyants can tap in to clairaudient practices to bolster their imaging techniques and interpretations. They can do this with their ability to envision. In this chapter I'm going to show you how to perform this maneuver, which will greatly expand your ability to assess clairvoyant insights. I will emphasize visual processes that allow you to use your clairvoyant abilities to perceive verbal information. I call this process "verbal visioning." (My next book in this series will feature clairaudience in all its configurations. You'll just have to wait to read some of the good stuff involved in clairaudience!)

I'll first explain the benefits of tapping in to your clairaudience to boost your clairvoyance, whether you are employing classical or prophetic clairvoyant skills. Then I'll explain how this process works biologically and energetically. I always think it's important to understand how a method operates. Information quiets the mind and allows our intuitive faculties to be more productive. I'll finish this chapter by outlining two useful exercises for connecting your psychic verbal capability with your visual acuity.

In this chapter you'll see that a few words—or verbal messages—might not be the equivalent of a thousand pictures, but they can sure help you figure out the story that a picture is trying to tell.

Capturing Meaning Through Words

A few years ago I had to decide if I should sell my rental house or not. The market had nose-dived and although I'd sell at a loss, I didn't want to manage another renter. I asked for a clairvoyant sign using the Seeking a Sign: The Everyday Vision Quest exercise featured in chapter 3.

I expected to receive a dream that evening or a psychic vision over the next few days. The message was even more astounding and involved a form of verbal visioning.

Within a few days of querying the Spirit, I started receiving dozens of mailers. Each was imprinted with the decree Sell Your House. Even more oddly—and aptly— the featured house looked nearly identical to my own. I sold my rental house and happily resigned from my landlord role.

As this example shows, clairvoyance and clairaudience can be closely intertwined, whether they are adjoined through our psychic or sensory abilities. When perceiving verbal signs through our clairvoyance, we're putting two powerful mystical gifts together. This relationship "doubles" the impact. We have twice the input necessary to excavate a vision.

As expressed in the introduction to this chapter, I'm not going to show you how to hear words, songs, conversations, and the like through your psychic or hearing senses. Instead, I'm going to help you "read" verbal insights.

In the previous house example, I revealed how you might read a message shown in the environment. You can go a step further and read verbal messages psychically.

For example, I once worked with a teenager who was wondering about her spiritual gifts. She was heading off to college and wanted assistance in selecting a major.

The first classical vision that I saw was bright red. I know that "red" people are energetic and passionate. They excel at physical activity, such as sports, and make productive use of the material world. As you might imagine, however, there are hundreds of different ways that someone who is physically gifted can hone and apply their innate traits.

Knowing that this young woman was looking for precise input, I asked the Spirit to add a few words so I could offer practical advice. Instantly I saw two words written like a caption underneath the clairvoyant image of the girl: Sports Performance. I shared this insight.

The girl laughed. She was a soccer player but knew that she wasn't good enough to go pro. She'd been thinking about majoring in sports coaching so she could eventually train athletes. The caption I had psychically received confirmed the path she was already considering.

I frequently request that clairaudient insights accompany clairvoyant images. Sometimes the clairaudient message appears as written words on, over, or under a picture, as exemplified in the example I just provided. There are other forms that these "verbal visions" can take as well. For instance, I once envisioned a picture of a client walking on a bridge. I knew that she was undergoing several painful transitions, including a divorce, a job loss, and the death of her mother, and that she was at a loss about how to manage her life going forward. So I asked for a verbal vision.

Immediately, lyrics unfolded underneath the psychic bridge scene. I recognized the song that they were from. One phrase was in bold script. Paraphrased, it stated the following: "Your heart's in San Francisco."

My client was considering a job offer in California. Given the lyrics, she took the job and moved. She had a session over the phone a few years later and shared that although her job had started in Los Angeles, she'd been transferred to San Francisco and loved her new life.

So far, the examples I've provided feature classical clairvoyance. You can also visualize verbal messages for prophetic visions. Imagine that you are focused on your seventh chakra and asking if you should get a pet. Imagine that you're shown a picture that's gray. Gray hues are the most difficult to interpret. Information lies hidden under the cloak of gray. *Okay*, you think. *I'll ask for a verbal clue.* You get one. A word forms under the image: Wait.

I had a client experience this exact situation. She wanted a pet, but the verbal vision indicated that she should wait. She did. About a year later she sent me an email. She had become the brand-new "mom" of her just-deceased grandmother's dog. My client was happy that she was able to accommodate the dog. If she had already owned a pet, she would have had to pass on adopting her grandmother's dog.

Following is a compilation of the various ways that verbal visions might appear. Included are encapsulations of the methods already described.

CAPTIONS: A great way to interpret psychic images is to request or receive captioning. Captions consist of words, phrases, or sentences imprinted on, above, or under a clairvoyant picture. You can also ask the Spirit to help you write words, drawings, or doodles on paper for additional clarity.

LYRICS, POEMS, BOOK PASSAGES, AND EVER SO MUCH MORE: Sometimes the Spirit or your guides will send psychic images of lyrics, poems, book passages, and even essays to help you interpret a vision. Of course, you could come across these in your everyday life as well. Imagine that you are thinking about a concern and a book falls open, the pages miraculously opening to a meaningful message. As well, you might psychically or physically be shown internet sites, academic journals, and the like as guideposts. I research my books using verbal visioning. I ask which internet sites might be helpful, and I'm shown a verbal vision.

ENVIRONMENTAL MESSAGES: Vision and verbal combine when you read words in the environment, an activity already discussed in chapter 1. Common environmental communiqués include billboards, mailers, emails, and license plates. For instance, I once saw a version of the word *love* on various license plates five times in one day. The promptings helped me realize how much love I had in my life.

———

How exactly do indicators from the clairaudient world meet up with those from the clairvoyant universe? Following a quick explanation of this matter, I'll walk you through two exercises that will help you integrate these mystical abilities.

The Meeting of the Minds

HOW CLAIRAUDIENCE WORKS WITH CLAIRVOYANCE

How do clairaudience and clairvoyance interact? The answer is found in biological and energetic explanations. Understanding this information will help you maximize this mystic partnership.

Biologically, science has proven that the auditory and visual systems frequently interact. In fact, perceptions gathered through one can be altered by the information taken in by another; the two systems are complementary.

Consider the results of several studies that have shown when both senses provide data about the same object or event, the resulting perception is more accurate. In fact, one sense will actually adjust or alter the conclusions of another. This means that if you add words to a picture, the meaning of the picture is enhanced. You'll arrive at a more apt conclusion.

What happens when you switch from one psychic vision to another, as I've been teaching you to do? Basically, as you change viewpoints, or the way you look at a subject, you receive different information from your verbal senses (Bulkin and Groh 2006). For the clairvoyant, this fact emphasizes why it's helpful to ask for additional visions when using your clairvoyance. Every time you seek a new psychic vision, you can also request a new verbal vision.

Not only are our visual and verbal senses interconnected biologically, but they are intertwined within the subtle energy system. Classical clairvoyance operates through the sixth chakra, and prophetic clairvoyance works through the seventh chakra. You have learned that the empathic senses, which involve chakras one through four, can be converted into sixth or seventh chakra images. Clairaudience is run by the fifth chakra, which is found in the throat area. Physical and subtle energies are easily exchanged between the fifth, sixth, and seventh chakras, as they are all near each other. Of course, you can also pass empathic sensations into the higher chakras and receive verbal visions for any type of message.

Are you ready to practice what I've been preaching? The following exercises will help you safely integrate verbal insights into your clairvoyant images.

Receiving a Psychic Verbal Vision

In this exercise you'll be shown how to open to a psychic verbal vision, which will utilize your clairaudient and clairvoyant abilities. You'll start with obtaining a psychic image. If you have a vision that came to you previously, I'll show you where to insert it during this exercise. Next, you'll request words, a lyric, or some other form of verbal vision to add clarification.

> PREPARE: Find a quiet space in which to be shepherded through this exercise. Come up with a particular question or concern and reflect upon it for a minute.

> STEP ONE: **Conduct Spirit-to-Spirit.** Affirm your personal spirit, that of all visible and invisible beings involved with this concern, and the Spirit.

> STEP TWO: **Request an Image.** Ask the Spirit to provide a clairvoyant image related to the sub-

ject at hand. If you've already obtained an image related to this issue, you can insert that image in your mind at this point. The image might qualify as a classical or a prophetic vision, or it might contain elements of both.

STEP THREE: **Analyze the Image.** Reflect upon the received image. Use the Q&A lists relayed at the end of previous chapters to analyze the important components.

STEP FOUR: **Add Clairaudience.** Ask the Spirit to provide a verbal message that you can visually perceive, one that will help explain the key image or images already provided. If you need a verbal vision beyond the one first provided, you can do the following:

- Ask the Spirit or your guides to write a caption on the main picture so you can understand it.

- Inquire if the Spirit will let you envision song lyrics related to your concern.

- Request that the Spirit show you a passage from a written work or show you where to find a printed message in the real world.

- Complete the analysis by putting all the
  components of your interactions together
  and running your conclusions by the Spirit.
  If you need more data, request it.

STEP FIVE: **Close.** Thank the Spirit and all the
helpers for the insights gained. Take a few deep
breaths and return to your everyday life when
ready.

Exercise
--18--

Verbal Visions in the Environment

MAKING MEANING OF THEM

What do you do if a verbal message flashes at you through
the environment? How about if your eye catches on a
billboard, a written work, or some other conveyance? If
you're confused, here are hints to figure out what the
message means.

Take a mental picture of the verbal vision and sit in a quiet place, then conduct Spirit-to-Spirit. You can use a piece of paper and pen or simply ponder the following questions or statements for insight:

- Is this really a verbal vision? (If not, you can quit the exercise right now.)

- Is this verbal sign meant for me? (If not, ask if you are supposed to receive and interpret the vision. Ask also who this verbal vision is aimed at, if you are supposed to analyze for the message, and if you should share your interpretation of the message with that person or not. If you aren't supposed to proceed, you can end this exercise right now.)

- Is the source of this message approved by the Spirit? (If not, you can end this exercise and ask the Spirit to cleanse you of any interference, cords, or other types of attachments that you are vulnerable to. Use healing streams to do this.)

- What subject does this verbal vision relate to? (If you were thinking about something or someone when you spotted this verbal message, simply double-check if the message pertains to that subject.)

- Now interpret the statement according to your common sense. Then ask, "Is this the correct interpretation?" If not, ask for an additional psychic vision—or verbal vision—to help you better understand the message.

- Ask if there is anything else you need to know about the message. For instance, you might ask if you should relay a message, take action, do further research, perform an additional meditation, or the like. Know that the Spirit can actually write all these answers on your mind screen to help you out. There isn't a limit to how many words you can receive.

Thank the Spirit and your helpers for giving you insights, then continue with your everyday activities.

Additional Tip

USING A SCENT OR A STONE

Return to chapter 3's Stones and Objects for Clairvoyance section (page 102) and Essential Oils for Clairvoyance section (page 105). You can always make use of stones or oils to enhance a verbal visioning process.

In particular, the violet and indigo stones are beneficial for cultivating clairvoyant and verbal visions. The fifth chakra is blue, which means that the bluer the stone, the more effectively the stone can enhance your verbal skills. You can hold the appropriate stone when focusing psychically or even wear it as jewelry.

You can use an essential oil to simultaneously enhance both your visual and verbal connectivity. From the short list provided on page 105, select an oil that suits your cause. For instance, if you sense an evil presence, consider using basil or fennel. If you want to enhance your bond with an angelic presence, employ frankincense.

———

Now that you've added yet another special skill to your clairvoyant tool kit, you are ready to learn about one of the most famous—and infamous—aspects of clairvoyance. Anyone ready for the future?

Additional Questions
ADDING TO YOUR QUEUE

Now you may add the following questions to your Q&A queue, which you've been creating since the end of chapters 2-5:

- Is it possible to receive captioning or verbal signs to better understand this psychic image?

- Can I receive a verbal vision with my eyes to help me out?

- Is the Spirit willing to help me write words on a picture to give me a needed message?

• • • • • • •

Summary

Clairvoyant images, whether classical or prophetic, can be better understood with insights provided through clairaudience. Clairaudience is a mystical gift that involves receiving messages that are verbal in nature. These can come through psychic or environmental means. As related to clairvoyance, obtaining "verbal visuals" can be particularly helpful.

In short, you can use your clairvoyant gifts to read messages pertaining to a picture or a vision. By seeing words, internet sites, lyrics, or other verbal messages on your psychic mind screen or through your eyes, you can more easily and deeply understand clairvoyant perceptions.

Clairvoyant Futuring
THE ART OF PREDICTING

Beyond a doubt, this is the most popular question that my clients ask: "What does my future hold?"

Clairvoyant futuring is a complex matter, which is why I've devoted an entire chapter to the subject. After sharing a few of the hundreds of ways that humans have attempted to predict the future across time, I'll next define several futuring terms. With a deeper understanding of this mainly prescriptive but sometimes descriptive capability, you'll understand why it's important to study it. When we peer through time's shadows, we can sometimes foresee what could, should, won't, shouldn't, mustn't, and will occur. Based on our perceptions, we make choices that determine future outcomes in this ring-around-the-rosy game.

I'll then outline the four basic types of futuring. To understand the meaning or accuracy of a futuristic vision, you must define it as a possibility, probability, certainty, or warning. I'll explain these terms and give advice for discerning between these types of visions. Then I'll share an exercise for performing futuring, which will draw on classical and prophetic insights. A list of additional tips will suggest ways to use this exercise to make effective decisions, employ futuristic journeying, use a scrying tool, and more.

Take out your crystal ball—it's time to gaze at the (potential) future!

Mirror, Mirror On the Wall
WHAT'S IN THE FUTURE FOR US ALL?

We humans have been extremely imaginative in our attempt to figure out the future. In the A's alone, we've conducted armomancy to guess at tomorrow by measuring the distance between the shoulders of beasts, augury to predict the future according to the flights of birds, and astrology to pinpoint events based on the movements of the stars. Robin Hood fans indulged in belomancy to figure out the future based on the flights of arrows, and fire mongers have employed ceromancy to perceive the patterns left by melting candles.

Want to know when you—or someone—might die? You could picture a "death clock," the image of which reveals the exact time and year of a passing, and if you're the active sort, you might try gyromancy, which involves walking in circles while querying the future. You can even employ parrots: ask a question and the pandering parrot will select a prewritten paper out of a container.

While everyday folks have used these and other measures to see into tomorrow, most cultures have also employed professionals. Labels for these practitioners include seer, intuitive, shaman, oracle, crystal-gazer, fortuneteller, intuitive, forecaster, augur, Sybil, futurist, soothsayer, psychic, and, of course, clairvoyant. No matter the term, there are literally hundreds of ways to formulate a prediction.

Not every futuring practice involves clairvoyance, yet I've discovered that almost every futuring technique can be adapted to the clairvoyant. In this chapter you'll be shown how to merge your clairvoyance and the following futuring styles:

DIVINING: Receiving futuristic information from the Spirit or divine messengers.

FORESIGHT: Psychically seeing what could or should occur.

FORETELLING: The act of speaking a desired future into existence.

FORTUNETELLING: Predicting what will create luck or take it away.

JOURNEYING: Visiting the future to help decide what to do today.

PRESENTIMENT: Also called precognition, this involves reading the body to empathically read the future.

SCRYING: The use of tools, including gemstones or water, to perceive what's to come.

These and all other futuring processes will essentially enable you to perform one or more of four basic futuring capabilities. If you want to know what your clairvoyance can actually reveal, take a look.

The Four Futures

My client loved his recurring dream but didn't understand why it hadn't come true. Nearly every week for years he dreamed that he would win the lottery. He consistently purchased lottery tickets, but he'd yet to win more than a couple of dollars. He was confused about why spiritual guidance would seemingly promise—but never deliver—a win.

As we've discussed throughout this book, a clairvoyant image could be a vision or a fantasy; it might also be literal or metaphorical. These distinctions apply to any clairvoyant picture or sign, including futuristic ones. They can also be prescriptive (hint at the future) or descriptive (ripe with advice). I led my client through a short guided exercise aimed at helping him obtain psychic images to explain the dream. He sighed. The first image he perceived showcased his friends and family. This image told him that his dream was descriptive and metaphorical, encouraging him to embrace the wealth in his relationships.

My client then received a second psychic image. It illustrated a lottery ticket. Maybe there was a prescriptive nature to his dream? The ticket in the vision was dim and wavy and near the border of the picture's edge; these factors hint that a psychic image is a possibility. We conducted Spirit-to-Spirit and used healing streams of grace, requesting that the Spirit transform the possibility into a probability if that outcome assured the highest good. In the resulting image, the lottery ticket was brighter and a bit more centered, which indicates that a possibility has transformed into a probability or at least a high possibility. And within a few months, my client did win a lottery— for one hundred dollars. He was delighted. To him, the win emphasized the involvement of God in his daily life.

There are four observations that can be indicated in a clairvoyant image, whether the vision is delivered classically or prophetically. These four categories are possibilities, probabilities, certainties, and warnings. The basic distinctions between these divisions are as follows:

Possibilities

A possibility is something that might happen. Possibilities occur on a curve, ranging from the nearly impossible to strong potentials. Most futuristic images or signs are possibilities. These insights can be useful. Based on knowing what's possible, we can avoid potential disasters or work harder toward a goal. We can also adjust our expectations by knowing what might—or might not—happen.

For example, a client wanted me to confirm that her boyfriend would marry her. After all, her clairvoyant images showed them marrying with her wearing a blue velvet dress. My own clairvoyant picture of my client's future in relation to her boyfriend was of her sitting on a couch watching movies alone. Perhaps her vision was a fantasy—either that or a mere possibility. I sensed in my gut that my own image was also just a possibility. I encouraged my client to work toward the dream of marriage but to be careful about expecting that her boyfriend shared the same outcome.

In the end, my client's boyfriend broke up with her. In the wake of their breakup she spent a lot of Friday evenings home alone. She said that her breakup was easier because she had already adjusted her expectations, thus proving a vital lesson in the prediction game: you can't control someone else. Dream big—but remember that there are many bends in the river.

Probabilities

Once a possibility strengthens, it transforms into a probability. This occurs when the near-infinite number of possibilities narrows to a handful. It's important to discern between possibilities and probabilities in order to save energy and to focus. For instance, my youngest son was looking at a number of colleges, aiming at a baseball scholarship. I prayed for guidance and kept seeing green and gold colors in my visions. I knew which school was branded with these colors. Although I didn't ignore the other schools, I did encourage my son to intelligently evaluate the green and gold school. In the end he accepted a scholarship at that school. I believe that following this prescriptive image with "descriptive" or intelligent actions helped determine the result.

Certainties

Sometimes an event or circumstance is just plain going to happen. I call these events "certainties," but also "destiny points," indicating that all possible and probable paths are leading to a specific juncture.

We agree to some certainties before birth, laying them out on our life path. Typical destiny points include the selection of parents, important relationships, health matters, and certain career possibilities, as well as accidents, illnesses, and heartbreaks. We make these agreements to clear our soul issues and learn about love and life. Not every destiny point occurs, however. Commonly clients ask why they haven't met their "soul mate" or why their soul mate married someone else. People (and all living beings) make decisions on the fly, and these not only alter the holder's contracts, but also impact everyone else involved in that contract.

In actuality, we plan many situations on the go. Because most life decisions are negotiated or decided within our subconscious, unconscious, spirit, or soul, we often aren't aware of the final agreements between ourselves and others. Clairvoyant processes can sometimes highlight the finalized conclusions, however. I've cultivated my gift so that I can sometimes perceive certainties years before they occur. I still remember a client calling me back five years after a session, sharing that the "pointed shoes" I saw on her eventual mate had showed up—her fiancé wore pointed cowboy boots. Most certainties, however, are imparted moments or maybe a day before they occur. In fact, studies have shown that a part of our mid-brain seems to predict events about five seconds before they happen, and that these predictions are correct about 90 percent of the time (Smith 2011). Yet other destiny points occur because of hard work. For instance, if you keep applying for jobs, you are bound to get one.

Many of my clients want a "for sure." There are far fewer certainties than probabilities and more possibilities than anything else. I have my own way of distinguishing between these three categories, which I'll share in the upcoming Future Factors section.

Warnings

Many futuristic images or signs are warnings or red flags. Warnings are tricky. No matter how frightening an image, it might be only a possibility. However, it could also be a probability or even a certainty.

To be warned about a possibility can be extremely helpful, as you might be able to avert trouble. For instance, I once received an image of a client losing his house to foreclosure. Literally, I saw a caption underneath the image: Foreclosure.

I asked my client if this was a possibility. He assured me that he paid his bills on time. "But does your husband?" I asked, glimpsing a clairvoyant image of a man throwing money out of a billfold. My client turned white. His husband was a gambling addict.

The two eventually divorced. My client didn't lose the house, however, because of the forewarning. He put together an in-marriage "prenuptial" and ended up with the house and none of his husband's debt.

Warnings can also be probabilities. Knowing about what's probable can help us alter a potentially negative situation, steer destiny toward a positive one, or help us cope if a hardship does occur. What happens, however, if the ultimate decision-making power lies with someone else? As a case in point, a client dreamed that her husband left her for another woman. The dream was vividly convincing, yet my client's gut suggested that there was wiggle room. My advice was to engage in therapy with her husband. They did. Even so, my client's husband left her for another woman within a couple of years.

Could my client's clairvoyant insight have been a certainty rather than a probability? Not in this case. Eventually the husband became dissatisfied with his new relationship and asked his wife to return to therapy with him. Over time, the couple reunited. If my client and her husband hadn't previously worked on their marriage in therapy, it probably would have permanently broken down.

Warnings that are certain are challenging because, by definition, we can't change them. It can even seem torturous to know a painful outcome in advance. I have a client who met a man and saw herself marrying him—but also divorcing him later. What was the point? Well, their son is an amazing individual.

The truth is that because of our human limitations, we don't know if a futuristic event will be good or bad, even if it's packaged as a warning. A for-sure marriage can crumble into an abysmal mire. A destiny-delivered death can help us face deeper issues and change us for the best. My own way of dealing with any clairvoyantly shared future is to ask the Spirit, "How am I to be with this?" We aren't promised a rose garden, but we can call upon the Master Gardener for help.

Future Factors

DISTINGUISHING BETWEEN POSSIBILITIES, PROBABILITIES, CERTAINTIES, AND WARNINGS

How can you tell the difference between possibilities, probabilities, certainties, and warnings? The ultimate answer is to know yourself. Everyone has a different style and understands their clairvoyance in a unique way. Having said that, I'd like to share what works for me.

First, you have to ascertain if a vision or sign pertains to the future rather than the present or the past. Sometimes it's hard to tell, especially if you are tuning in to a person you don't know. I analyze psychic visions for their futuristic factors in these ways:

A PURPLE HUE: Purple is the color of the sixth chakra but also of the future. In a classical image, purple tints usually indicate a future potential.

DISTANCING: If the action, main focus, or major figure in a classical image is near the image's border, that scene could relate to the future. Likewise, in a prophetic vision, a bright white image located far away from a vision's center could be futuristic.

OUTSIDE OF THE AURIC FIELD: If you can psychically picture a being with an auric field and the
major activity in the image is occurring outside of the field, that event hasn't yet landed in
everyday reality.

SPARKLES: When I spy sparkles outside of someone's energy field, whether with my eyes or in a
vision, something exciting is about to happen.

VERBAL CUES: If you don't know what time period
a vision relates to, ask for captions or another
verbal cue.

FEELING: Sometimes a clairvoyant image or sign
simply feels futuristic, so go with it. If you can't
tell, evaluate for the sensations described in
chapter 5 and imagine that the indicator relates
to the past, present, and the future, in that order.
Your body will let you know which is correct.

ENVIRONMENTAL SIGNS: If a clairvoyant prompt
comes through the environment and you sense
it's futuristic, ask for two more environmental
indications to confirm that the sign applies to
the future. Also conduct Spirit-to-Spirit and ask
for a psychic image to reveal the related time

period. If a potentially futuristic image comes in a psychic vision, ask for an environmental sign or conduct a vision quest, as you were shown how to do in chapter 3, to prove it's futuristic. Decide what would need to be revealed to substantiate the vision as futuristic in your mind.

ASK THE OTHER PERSON: If you are attuning for another person, ask them if they think that the sign or psychic image you've received (or they've received) is futuristic or otherwise.

PROPHETIC/CLASSICAL BLEND: When I'm confused about the time period related to an image or sign, I use Spirit-to-Spirit and request a hybrid psychic picture. I divide my mind screen into two parts, black on the left side and white on the right side, which establishes a prophetic backdrop. Then I ask that a classical image appear on the dark side to reveal the darkest of possible futures related to an issue. I request that a classical image appear on the white side to show the best possible future related to the same issue. This is a great process for making decisions with the future in mind.

WARNINGS: Use any of the above tools to figure out if a warning relates to the future or not.

After I know that an image relates to the future, I further catalogue the clairvoyant perception and work with it in the following ways:

Possibilities

Possibilities look like this:

- Events or main figures are located in the farthest edges of an image's border or away from a main figure's auric field. It's the same with a sign: possibilities will show up geographically far away from you.

- The main action or central image is wavy, dim, or hard to distinguish.

- There are so many images or signs you can't select a dominant one; you are probably perceiving a number of possibilities.

- For prophetic images, the main focus is gray or encased in gray, indicating that an event hasn't landed or differentiated yet, or that you aren't supposed to know a determined outcome.

- Empathically, you feel confused or like the plausibility of the perception is questionable.

- Your bodily sensations are perplexing and unclear about the likelihood of a potential future
  happening.

Regarding my latter point, I've learned that the body is king. Even when a client presses me to assure them that a happy future picture or sign is "for sure," I don't go there if my body won't. For instance, a client asked if she would be hired by a particular modeling agency. I received a dimly lit psychic picture that wasn't clear. My body was confused as well, so I told the client that I wasn't certain. She was unhappy with my statement, but I couldn't alter the picture or my feelings. In fact, she wasn't hired by that agency but rather by a different one. It always pays to be honest with your clairvoyance.

What if you want to "guarantee" that a possibility evolves into a probability or certainty? Good luck with that! While we might be able to influence an outcome, we can't control the many streams of life, especially if an endeavor involves other people. You can always request healing streams of grace and ask that the Spirit secure the highest outcome. Then let go and do your part to turn a possibility into something stronger. If you want a better job, work harder. If you want to meet a mate, join a dating site.

Probabilities

These tend to energetically look like this:

- The main focus of an image is clear and distinct but not centered in the picture. It might be skewed to the side. An environmental sign might be near you but not terribly close geographically.

- From an auric field point of view, the message conveying the probability is near a being's energy field but not actually inside the field, body, or chakra.

- You're gripped with a keen sense that something could or even should occur, but you aren't firmly convinced.

- With prophetic images, the central feature is whitish gray.

As indicated, sometimes a probability can be upgraded or downgraded. Most obviously, you want to transform a positive probability into more of a certainty and a negative probability into a mere possibility, or get rid of the latter altogether. Sometimes you can effect change, but, of course, life doesn't only concern itself with you or another's dreams and desires. For instance, I once worked with a client who was flying to Jamaica. I kept seeing an image of his plane crash-landing. He'd had the same vision in his dreams. I didn't know how strong the future potential was, so I asked the Spirit to transform the classical image into a prophetic one. The plane turned whitish gray, which marks a probability. There was more gray than white, though, which meant that we could perhaps influence the outcome. I asked for healing streams of grace to bring about a better outcome. The crash didn't occur. The plane did lose an engine, however, but it was still able to land.

Certainties

These are rendered in the following ways:

- The main message is square in the middle of a main character's body or energetic system, or in the center of the image's frame. However, if the featured message is inside of the auric field, it's still on the way but will land. If environmental, the harbinger or sign will be obvious and geographically close.

- They are accompanied by a knowing so strong, the awareness leaves no doubt.

- The image moves you to action, even if you don't logically understand why.

An authentic certainty can't be avoided. Years ago I awoke with the image of a store to visit. A caption under the vision said Boyfriend. I went to the store, and a future boyfriend was there. Regardless, the Spirit can intervene in any situation. I once prayed for an eighty-year-old Christian client who had suffered a heart attack. She had been given two weeks to live, and the image presented me was of her death. As always, however, I turned the outcome over to the Spirit—and her cardiovascular system grew new blood vessels. She lived another year. Was the image I received only a probability? We don't always know. We can, however, ask for higher assistance.

Warnings

Warnings will meet these criteria:

- They will leave you scared or frightened.
- They seem real, like the event is already occurring.
- Warnings can be either negative or positive. Sometimes happy events can frighten us too! For instance, we might dream of having a child and become scared. Maybe our own childhood wasn't so good; maybe we're frightened about the birthing pain.
- Warnings could pertain to yourself or another.

Upon receiving a warning, follow the protocol involved in differentiating between possibilities, probabilities, and certainties. This will establish how serious the upcoming situation might be. But first, make sure that the warning pertains to you or the person you are checking in for. Sometimes a portent belongs to someone else, hence the need for the subtle boundaries we discussed in chapter 2. Look also for energetic attachments, which we discussed in chapter 3. Future events meant for a co-contract holder can get transferred to another.

For example, I once worked with a client who most likely absorbed the illness meant for his twin brother, who had been exhibiting symptoms before my client came down with them. As soon as my client became sick, the illness symptoms disappeared in the brother.

At first, my client wouldn't release the illness, as he didn't want to sicken his brother. Both my client and myself clairvoyantly perceived one or the other dying of the disease. Using the healing process that you'll learn in the next chapter, we released the entire issue from my client and his brother's spirit. My client became well and his brother stayed well.

Also, double-check the source of a message. Interfering entities sometimes try to scare people in order to stir up and steal the resulting emotional energy. Ask for signs or psychic images to double-check an image's source, and use the Healing Streams of Grace technique to release yourself from anything unhealthy, such as cords or interference. As always, if a warning seems highly certain and negative, ask for healing streams to provide assistance.

Drawing on all the advice just provided, you can use the following exercise to obtain psychic images of the future.

Exercise
—19—

Clairvoyant Foresight
SEEING THE FUTURE

Do you want to obtain or understand a classical or prophetic futuring vision or sign? Do you need to make a decision? This exercise will help you with those goals. You'll assess a vision or sign as prescriptive or descriptive (or both); figure out if the image reflects a possibility, probability, certainty, or warning; shift one type of vision into another (if desirable or possible), and, if pertinent, make a decision.

PREPARE: Settle into a comfortable space and breathe deeply.

STEP ONE: **Conduct Spirit-to-Spirit.** Affirm your own spirit, the helping spirits, and the Spirit.

STEP TWO: **Engage a Psychic Vision.** There are several options:

- Concentrate on a question or issue and ask for a psychic vision, either classical or prophetic, to provide futuristic insight.

- Select a previously received psychic vision or sign you'd like futuristic information about.

- Request a futuristic image that the Spirit wants to send you right now.

STEP THREE: **Double Check the Image.** Use the factors provided in this chapter to double-check that the image relates to the future. You can assess landscape placement, the key figure, and coloration and brightness, and also evaluate with your empathic sensations. Ask too for verbal input if needed. Before proceeding, make sure the image or sign is genuine rather than fantasy, and check for other factors including sourcing. If you don't relate to the vision, use healing streams of grace to release it and ask for another one.

STEP FOUR: **Assess for Type.** Figure out if the vision is a possibility, probability, certainty, or warning. Use the tools already taught in this chapter. The basic differences are that classical possibilities are dim, distant, and feel questionable; a probability is stronger, more focused, and brighter; a certainty will grab you and be "in your face"; and a warning will feel foreboding and can be further subcategorized as a possibility, probability, or certainty. Prophetic possibilities are feature images that are farther away and gray; probabilities are white-gray and closer in; and certainties are bright white and front and center.

STEP FIVE: **Dig for Meaning.** Now use the questions and concerns already shared in this book to assess the vision. What is the main message? What is it telling you? Do you need another image to interpret the message? Use the tools already featured in this book, such as evaluating color, locations, shapes, numbers, point of view, sources, and more. Besides the prescriptive nature of the image or sign, check for descriptive points, such as advice or insight. You can always ask for additional images, change points of view, request captions, and use other tools to perform your evaluation.

STEP SIX: **Take Action.** If the image is a possibility, what should you do? How about if it's a probability or a certainty? Ask for additional images and verbal insights to respond to these and similar questions. Also request healing streams of grace to assist with healthy change.

STEP SEVEN: **Close.** When you feel finished, take a few deep breaths and thank the Spirit for the help.

Additional Tips

MAKING MORE OF THE FUTURE

I've already sprinkled tips throughout this chapter for making more of your future insights. Here are additional ideas that will help you walk in the footsteps of clairvoyant greats. Many of these suggestions are adapted from the list of futuring processes outlined earlier in this chapter.

EXPAND THE IMAGE: Want to see more in a frame? This "reverse-zooming" technique will reveal more details. It works best with a classical image. Simply ask the Spirit to push out the borders of the vision. Ask that the expanded landscape be populated with figures, symbols, or characters that will help you better understand the future image—it's likelihood and malleability, in particular.

MIX PRESCRIPTIVE AND DESCRIPTIVE: Futuring is basically a prescriptive action, showing what could occur. Descriptive images will offer suggestions for action. You can receive both types of insights with your clairvoyance. After better defining a prescriptive image, ask for descriptive insights to showcase choices. For instance, if you receive a vision inferring that you won't get a desirable job, ask for pictures that might reveal what jobs to apply for.

DIVINE DIRECTLY: When divining, we specifically work with the Spirit or its direct assistants, such as the angels, masters, or the divinely approved deceased, for insight. When conducting the Clairvoyant Foresight: Seeing the

Future exercise, ask that an angel, master, the Spirit, or another high-level being interact with you. Ask to psychically perceive them. Ask that their name be shared in a caption or that their message be inscribed within lyrics. Request too that the guide appears in your nightly dreams or daydreams to give guidance or alter future potentials for the highest good.

SEEK A FORETELLING: Foretelling involves speaking a desire into existence. Use this clairaudient gift by envisioning a caption under the image of a desirable future.

ADD LUCK: Fortunetelling adds or subtracts luck. Many Chinese medical systems propose that luck is an actual energy. When working with a desirable future image or sign, ask the Spirit to insert the energy of luck into the picture via healing streams of grace. Visualize the result of this additional good fortune.

JOURNEY TO THE FUTURE: Visiting a possible future can help you make decisions about today. Conduct Spirit-to-Spirit and concentrate on a futuristic concern. Ask that the Spirit help you picture all possible outcomes. Select the one that is the best for all. How do you know? Ask that the Spirit shower the most desirable future with white light or sparkles. Then ask for an expanded vision or a new picture that will reveal the keys to locking in that best future. What steps do you need to take or avoid? Use healing streams of grace to secure the energy of the futuristic pictures in your current self.

BODY READING: Presentiment allows your body to sense the future. Psychically envision a possible future and then sense your body's response. Does it feel pain or ease? Frustrated or happy? Keep scrolling through possible action steps and futuristic ideas and follow your body's guidance in deciding what to go for.

TRY SCRYING: Select a clear quartz, a crystal ball, or fill a bowl with water. Gaze at this iridescent tool while working futuristically. You probably won't perceive an image in the tool; rather, it will help illuminate the images inside of you and brighten the received clairvoyant images.

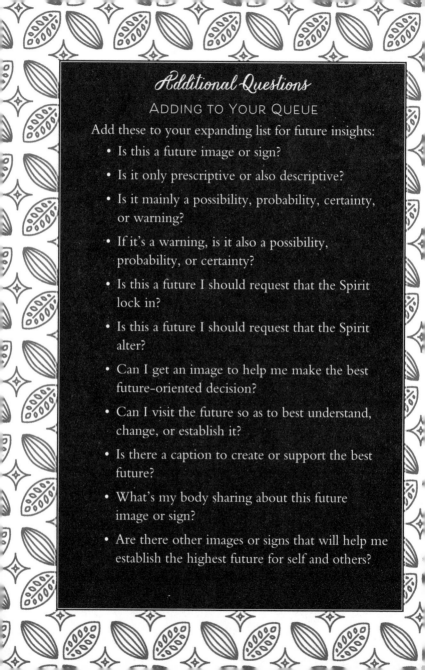

Additional Questions
ADDING TO YOUR QUEUE

Add these to your expanding list for future insights:

- Is this a future image or sign?

- Is it only prescriptive or also descriptive?

- Is it mainly a possibility, probability, certainty, or warning?

- If it's a warning, is it also a possibility, probability, or certainty?

- Is this a future I should request that the Spirit lock in?

- Is this a future I should request that the Spirit alter?

- Can I get an image to help me make the best future-oriented decision?

- Can I visit the future so as to best understand, change, or establish it?

- Is there a caption to create or support the best future?

- What's my body sharing about this future image or sign?

- Are there other images or signs that will help me establish the highest future for self and others?

Now that you have a sense of how to step into tomorrow, you'll make a final stop on our tour of clairvoyance. Two of the most powerful ways to apply clairvoyance are toward healing and manifesting, or releasing what doesn't work and attracting what is desired.

* * * * * * *
Summary

Humans have constantly sought glimpses of the future, seeking indications of what could, would, should, or shouldn't occur. Across time, plans have been established based on what is perceived through classical or prophetic clairvoyance or signs. In this chapter you learned several futuring terms and the differences between possibilities, probabilities, certainties, and warnings. You practiced a basic exercise for calling forth, analyzing, and working with futuristic insights and were given a few tips to expand your ability.

Here is to your future!

Healing and Manifesting Through Clairvoyance

When all is good, we are relaxed and take our lives a moment at a time. When we're out of alignment, there are two activities that clairvoyance can assist us with. These are healing and manifesting.

After defining these two terms, you'll engage with your healer self. Healing involves releasing whatever is preventing that which is beneficial. Think of how many life challenges stem from perceptions, memories, and wounds that are too powerful.

The other side of the coin is manifesting. To manifest is to invite or lock in what is desirable. Sometimes we can't manifest unless we perform healing first, removing blockages preventing the new from landing. But other times nothing is in the way—we can simply attract our desires to us. In this chapter you'll learn how to perform both maneuvers.

This chapter differs a bit from the others in that I'm going to jump right into the exercises. The first exercise focuses on healing and will involve using clairvoyance for retrocognition (assessing the past), the most typical source of our problems. In the exercise you'll deal with attachments and access a parallel reality for assistance. Additional tips will help you to connect with the deceased, perform a chakra/field reading, and send a vision to another for healing purposes.

The second exercise is aimed at helping you manifest. Part of this exercise will assist you with magnetizing, a term I use to describe the manifesting process that doesn't first require a healing process. All in all, this chapter will bring balance to your clairvoyant practice and life.

Exercise
--20--

Clairvoyant Healing

WORKING THROUGH YOUR HISTORY

Most of our current challenges originate in the past. Our history determines our current attitudes, beliefs, and emotions, as well as many of our activities, needs, and body issues. Psychic clairvoyance, whether classical or prophetic, is an ideal process for clarifying and clearing the origin of a problematic issue. In this exercise you'll use several of the tools already described in this book to peer into the past, analyze its effects, and release the resulting problems and blocks. The follow-on tips will help you adapt this exercise for differing purposes.

PREPARE: Breathe deeply and settle into a comfortable position. Make sure that you won't be disturbed.

STEP ONE: **Conduct Spirit-to-Spirit.** Acknowledge your personal spirit, the spirits of those involved in your past as well as your current spiritual guides, and the Spirit.

STEP TWO: **Concentrate on an Issue.** Think of a challenging issue and reflect upon it for a moment.

STEP THREE: **Locate the Origin.** Ask the Spirit to reveal the issue's cause. First ask for a classical image or series of images revealing a time period, situation, event, and characters. Feel any feelings that arise for you through this revelation, and sense how the past is still affecting you. Check for attachments that incurred because of this situation or that might have caused it. If you

· · · ·

sense that there are attachments and you can't perceive them through classical imagery, ask for a prophetic image. The attachments will be black, as will the areas they connect into your own or another's system.

STEP FOUR: **Clear the Attachments.** If there are attachments, request that the Spirit send healing streams of grace through the attachments and into all parties. If you are interested, ask the Spirit to clarify the reasons for the attachments and how they've impacted you. This information might be delivered as additional images, empathic understandings, or verbal assists.

STEP FIVE: **Search a Parallel Reality/Request Grace.** Remember, clairvoyance is highly adaptable to different time periods. In this step, request that the Spirit reveal a parallel or concurrent reality in which you are unaffected by the causal predicament—in other words, a picture of the healed self or situation. Assess the follow-on images. What's different about the self that isn't injured from the past? What does that self understand that your current self does not? As you reflect upon these questions, ask the self in that image to send you the healing streams of grace needed to clear up the historical trauma. As you receive these, ask the Spirit to send them through you and also into your past self. Then swim back into present-day time.

STEP SIX: **Close.** Feel your body's responses to the changes that are being delivered. Remain in this integration period as long as you need, and know that it will continue safely in your everyday life. Decide that you will be kind and loving to yourself while you adapt to all transformations. Breathe deeply, then return to your life.

Additional Tips

HEALING THROUGH CLAIRVOYANCE

Want to super-focus your clairvoyant healing? Here are a few additional means.

Interacting with the Deceased

Sometimes the deceased, including our ancestors, can relay a perspective necessary to our healing. And sometimes a deceased being, whether linked to a past or a current life, might be the injurious party. If you feel like a deceased being is causing or sustaining a block, ask for an image from or related to the deceased in step three, "Locate the Origin," in the previous exercise. Continue to interact with images related to this being until you are clear about its relationship with the issue. You'll also work with other causal images in addition to these.

Checking the Chakras and Auric Field

When conducting the healing exercise, you can insert an action between step two, "Concentrate on an Issue," and step four, "Clear the Attachments." Request that the Spirit reveal what is occurring within your chakras and auric field. Evaluate the shape and state of your chakras and auric fields. Probe the vision as you would any other clairvoyant image, requesting additional images if needed. Additional images related to your chakras and field might now appear in subsequent visions. For instance, you might notice attachments in a chakra or auric field or discover what your chakras and field will look like when healthy in the parallel reality. Working on these subtle systems can exponentially enhance your healing work.

Sending a Vision

If working on someone else, you will receive a vision of their healed self when evaluating their parallel reality. Ask for healing streams of grace to energize this healthy image and to then send it to the other's spirit. Their personal spirit will infuse their body, mind, and soul with the healing energy in ways best suited to them.

Exercise
-21-

Manifesting and Magnetizing Clairvoyantly

Who doesn't want to attract more good stuff into their lives? "Manifesting" is the code word used to describe the process involved in helping dreams come true. There are two ways to attract our desires. Traditional or standard manifesting involves first healing the blocks so we can then draw desires to us. "Magnetizing," however, describes manifesting as a one-step process. When magnetizing, you are recognizing that there isn't anything in the way of attracting your needs, and if there are impediments or issues, they are naturally worked through after the desire arrives in your life. You'll be provided the opportunity to try both processes in this exercise.

PREPARE: Find a quiet place in which to relax.

STEP ONE: **Conduct Spirit-to-Spirit.** Affirm your own spirit, the helping spirits, and the Spirit.

STEP TWO: **Frame Your Desire.** What would you like to draw into your life? Frame the need as a classical picture, letting yourself see and feel all aspects of the picture. If you want, write a caption underneath the image that summarizes your desire.

STEP THREE: **Select a Path.** What process will help you best create and attract your desire? Choice A, covered next, involves manifesting involving healing. Choice B focuses on magnetizing, which doesn't require healing. Are you confused about which process to undertake? Request a prophetic image showcasing Choice A and then one for Choice B. Select the image—and therefore, path—that is brightest and whitest.

- **Choice A: Perform Manifesting with Healing.** Run through exercise 20 to release the blocks preventing you from achieving your dream. Then ask the Spirit to infuse the portrait of your desire with healing streams of grace. Request images that will inform you about action steps to take. When you feel finished, take a few deep breaths and move to step four.

- **Choice B: Perform Magnetizing.**
Magnetizing is simple: concentrate on the
vision of your desire and ask the Spirit
to infuse that image into your auric field.
Using first- or second-person point of
view, watch as your field is imprinted with
the image. You might perceive it being
seared into the field or psychically see a
word representing the desire printed on
the outer border of your energetic field.
Simultaneously, you'll feel the energy and
emotion of your wish integrate into your
body. Simply accept this blessing.

STEP FOUR: **Close.** Return to the original image
representing your desire. Now see it in your
mind's eye. The empathic senses are a vital part
of transforming dreams into reality. Let yourself
feel, in every part of your being, the realness of
this wish. Imagine that your desire has actually
come true, and feel gratitude toward your own
spirit, the helping spirits, and the Spirit. Then
take a few deep breaths and return to your
everyday life.

Additional Questions
ADDING TO YOUR QUEUE

What healing and manifesting questions can help you with your clairvoyant practices? I'm adding the following to the mix:

- Is this situation in need of healing or release?

- What images will help me release what must be released? (I can also ask for healing streams of grace.)

- Am I in need of attracting a desire or need?

- What images will assist me in manifesting a need, which requires performing energetic release as well?

- What images will assist me in simply magnetizing my desire to me?

• • • • • • •
Summary

Healing involves releasing what has become a block or unnecessary energy. Manifesting is the code word for attracting desires to us. There are actually two types of manifesting. The mothership of manifesting requires that we first release what is creating a resistance to making a dream come true. After healing, the dream becomes more tangible. Magnetizing, on the other hand, skips the first step. We simply attract a desire and then work through any blocks while we're enjoying the gain.

Clairvoyance is a practical and powerful means for performing healing and manifesting.

CONCLUSION

Since time began, mystics have employed clairvoyance to see beyond the range of natural vision. Long ago, both royal and everyday seekers would travel great geographical distances to consult with famous augurs, seers, oracles, Sybils, or clairvoyants. These days, we don't have to trek over mountains or ford streams to benefit from psychic sight. We now recognize clairvoyance as an innate ability that is available to everyone. (And maybe many ancient cultures knew the same.)

Clairvoyance is one of several mystical abilities, but what a powerful one! Basically, it involves receiving messages visually. The process is ultimately energetic, which means it relies upon both physical and subtle energetic exchanges, employing our physical system and our subtle anatomy. Both our "normal" eyes and the "eyes" of our chakras and auric layers receive and create clairvoyant images.

Via the clairvoyant training that is the heart of this book, you learned about—and practiced—six different clairvoyant styles. What are these styles? A recap:

- Classical clairvoyant images are packaged as colorful psychic visions, nightly dreams and daydreams, and environmental signs.

- Prophetic visions appear as black to white psychic images.

- Empathic sensations can be transformed into images.

- Verbal insights also may be obtained in picture form.

- We may receive futuristic visions.

- We may apply clairvoyance through healing and manifesting.

As you moved through this book, you acquired a library of clairvoyant techniques. Who knew that there were so many ways to interpret a psychic or worldly vision? By applying the basic practices of Spirit-to-Spirit and Healing Streams of Grace, you figured out how to analyze a visual message for all sorts of insights, including

- fantasy or reality
- literal or metaphor

- prescription versus description
- point of view
- colors, shapes, and symbols
- locations and more

You were taught to create captions and lyrics on your mind screen, to feel into your bodily sensations, and so much more.

Ultimately, you were invited into the journey of your own personal development, for isn't that the true purpose of clairvoyance? It is a gift of light and bestows nothing more or less than a process for enlightenment.

Questions for Clairvoyant Analysis

Following is a collection of the questions shared at the end of chapters 2 through 8. These were specifically designed to enable you to use the clairvoyance practices and skills taught in their related chapters. I've collected them in one place so that you can assess the simplest or most complicated of visions and delve deeply into its meaning and message. I've slightly altered the appearance of a few of the questions so that they flow better in this form.

Your responses to the questions can come in many ways. The original image might change. You could receive a second picture. A classical image might convert into a prophetic picture. You could see a sign in the environment, or a sign might be understood through a psychic vision. Empathic or verbal information might also be added to the classical or prophetic indications.

With that, following are the questions you can employ to analyze a clairvoyant vision:

- Is this vision one I wanted to receive or is it just popping in? (voluntary or involuntary)

- If this image is involuntarily received, should I use Spirit-to-Spirit to further analyze it or not?

- Is this an actual vision or a fantasy? (visions cannot be altered; fantasies can)

- Is this image literal or metaphorical? (literal versus figurative)

- Who or what is showing me these images? (sourcing)

- Is this a Spirit-approved source of images? (sourcing)

- Is there a more Spirit-approved source of images that can help me psychically? (sourcing)

- Can I see more of the image? (full sight)

- Can I hone in on the most vital part of the image? (half sight)

- Through what point of view am I perceiving this image? (first person, second person, third-person limited, third-person omniscient)

- Is there a better point of view for understanding this image? (first person, second person, third-person limited, third-person omniscient)

- Is this image revealing an important idea? (insight)

- Is this picture about right now? (current sight)

- Is this vision about the past? (back sight, hindsight)

- Is this vision about the future? (foresight; further questions related to futuring are offered later in this list)

- Is this vision related to the future or right now? (prescriptive or descriptive)

- Can I receive another image to help interpret this one?

- Am I supposed to take an action based on this image?

- Is someone else supposed to take an action based on this insight?

- If this image relates to someone else, should I mention it? If so, how?

- Can I receive more information to clarify the following?

  * characters (people, beings, objects, props, etc.)

  * interactions

- ★ time period
- ★ interpretations of elements
- Can I be shown or told what other questions I should ask?
- Can I receive more information to clarify the following?
  - ★ colors:
    - − *clear colorations*
    - − *"off" colorations*
  - ★ attachments, such as cords or curses
  - ★ symbols:
    - − *shapes*
    - − *numbers*
  - ★ locations:
    - − *landscapes—environmental*
    - − *bodily*
    - − *chakric/field*
    - − *any others that stand out*
  - ★ supportive tools to use:
    - − *foods*
    - − *stones/objects*
    - − *oils*
  - ★ additional elements

- Would it be helpful to transform a classical clairvoyant image into a prophetic image or vice versa?

- If this image is prophetic, I request to be shown another image to explain these hues:

  * black

  * white

  * gray

- Should I be working empathically with my clairvoyance?

  * Are the empathic sensations I'm feeling someone else's?

  * Are the empathic sensations I'm feeling messages from spiritual sources?

  * Are the empathic sensations I'm experiencing from myself to myself?

  * Are there emotions, feelings, or understandings that can be turned into pictures to help me out?

    – *Are they physical in nature?*

    – *Are they feelings-based in nature?*

    – *Are they mental in nature?*

    – *Are they relational in nature?*

    – *Are they a mix of the four empathic styles?*

- Is it possible to receive captioning or verbal signs to better understand this psychic image?

- Can I receive a verbal vision with my eyes to help me out?

- Is the Spirit willing to help me write words on a picture to give me a needed message?

- Is this a future image or sign?

- Is it only prescriptive or also descriptive?

- Is it mainly a possibility, probability, certainty, or warning?

- If it's a warning, is it also a possibility, probability, or certainty?

- Is this a future I should request that the Spirit lock in?

- Is this a future I should request that the Spirit alter?

- Can I get an image to help me make the best future-oriented decision?

- Can I visit the future so as to best understand, change, or establish it?

- Is there a caption to create or support the best future?

- What's my body sharing about this future image or sign?

- Are there other images or signs that will help me establish the highest future for self and others?

- Is this situation in need of healing or release?

- What images will help me release what must be released? (I can also ask for healing streams of grace)

- Am I in need of attracting a desire or need?

- What images will assist me in manifesting a need, which requires performing energetic release as well?

- What images will assist me in simply magnetizing my desire to me?

- And finally, one more time, the most essential question: Is there anything else that the Spirit wants to show me?

Appendix B

Useful Information

Basic Chakras

- first—physical
- second—emotional
- third—mental
- fourth—relational
- fifth—verbal
- sixth—visual
- seventh—spiritual

Chakras eight through twelve are described in the first book in this series, *Subtle Energy Techniques*.

Types of Clairvoyance and Chakra Connections

- classical clairvoyance—sixth chakra
  - ★ psychic vision
  - ★ night dreams and daydreams
  - ★ environmental signs
- prophetic clairvoyance—seventh chakra
- emotional clairvoyance—second, third, and fourth chakras
- verbal clairvoyance—fifth
- futuring—can use all chakras
- healing and manifesting—can use all chakras

Chakras eight to twelve, described in first book of the series, can be clairvoyantly accessed through all the techniques in this book.

Easy Psychic Visioning Steps

- ask a question
- conduct Spirit-to-Spirit
  - ★ affirm personal spirit
  - ★ affirm others' spirits
  - ★ affirm the Spirit
- request a psychic vision
- analyze psychic vision or request additional visions
- ask for healing streams of grace to clear negativity
- close

REFERENCES

Bennett, D. M. 1881. *The Gods and Religions of Ancient and Modern Times, Volume II.* New York: D. M. Bennett, 306–308.

Bulkin, David A., and Jennifer M. Groh. 2006. "Seeing Sounds: Visual and Auditory Interactions in the Brain." Sciencedirect.com. http://people.duke.edu/~jmgroh/Bulkin_Groh_CurrOpNeuro2006.pdf.

Chia, Mantak, and Joyce Thom. 2016. "Opening the Third Eye." *Conscious Lifestyle Magazine.* http://www.consciouslifestylemag.com/pineal-gland-activation-third-eye/.

Dennis, M. K. August 25, 2010. "The Three Dreams of Renee Descartes." Splatter. https://marilynkaydennis.wordpress.com/2010/08/25/the-three-dreams-of-rene-descartes/.

Hill, J. 2008. "The Eye." Ancient Egypt Online. http://www.ancientegyptonline.co.uk/eye.html.

Hill, J. 2016. "Wadjet." Ancient Egypt Online. http://www.ancientegyptonline.co.uk/wadjet.html.

Quantumbiologist. September 25, 2010. "Third Eye." https://quantumbiologist.wordpress.com/2010/09/25/third-eye/.

Roney-Douglas, S. M. 2012. "Tibetan Psychic Traditions." Psi Research Centre. http://www.psi-researchcentre .co.uk/article_5.htm.

Smith, Graham. August 23, 2011. "We CAN predict the future (a bit): Why the brain knows what's going to happen before it does." Dailymail.com. http://www .dailymail.co.uk/sciencetech/article-2029189/We-CAN -predict-future-The-brain-knows-whats-going-happen -does.html.

Order at
LLEWELLYN
.COM

Prices subject to change without notice

Subtle Energy Techniques

BOOK 1 OF CYNDI DALE'S
ESSENTIAL ENERGY LIBRARY

Cyndi Dale

Renowned author Cyndi Dale invites you into the world of subtle energy, where you'll explore auras, chakras, intuition, and the basics of her groundbreaking energy techniques. Whether your goals are physical, psychological, or spiritual, these methods can help you achieve your desires, heal your wounds, and live an enlightened life.

978-0-7387-5161-0
5 X 7 · 288 PP. · $14.99

Order at
LLEWELLYN
.COM

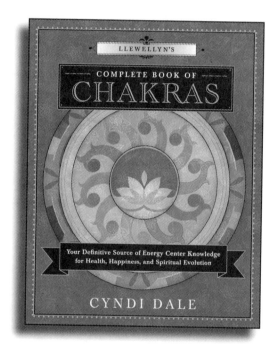

LLEWELLYN'S

COMPLETE BOOK OF

CHAKRAS

Your Definitive Source of Energy Center Knowledge
for Health, Happiness, and Spiritual Evolution

CYNDI DALE

Llewellyn's Complete Book of Chakras

YOUR DEFINITIVE SOURCE OF ENERGY
CENTER KNOWLEDGE FOR HEALTH,
HAPPINESS, AND SPIRITUAL EVOLUTION

Cyndi Dale

As powerful centers of subtle energy, the chakras have fascinated humanity for thousands of years. *Llewellyn's Complete Book of Chakras* is a unique and empowering resource that provides comprehensive insights into these foundational sources of vitality and strength. Discover what chakras and chakra systems are, how to work with them for personal growth and healing, and the ways our understanding of chakras has transformed throughout time and across cultures.

Lively and accessible, this definitive reference explores the science, history, practices, and structures of our subtle energy. With an abundance of illustrations and a wealth of practical exercises, Cyndi Dale shows you how to use chakras for improving wellness, attracting what you need, obtaining guidance, and expanding your consciousness.

978-0-7387-3962-5
8 X 10 · 1,056 PP. · $39.99